The Pastor
of New Mexico

The Pastor of New Mexico
Peter Küppers's Memoirs

Translated, Edited, and Annotated
Tomas Jaehn

SANTA FE

© 2014 by Tomas Jaehn
All Rights Reserved.

No part of this book may be reproduced in any form or by any electronic or mechanical means including information storage and retrieval systems without permission in writing from the publisher, except by a reviewer who may quote brief passages in a review.

Sunstone books may be purchased for educational, business, or sales promotional use. For information please write: Special Markets Department, Sunstone Press, P.O. Box 2321, Santa Fe, New Mexico 87504-2321.

Book and cover design › Vicki Ahl
Body typeface › Times New Roman
Printed on acid-free paper
∞
eBook 978-1-61139-303-3

Library of Congress Cataloging-in-Publication Data

Küppers, Peter, 1885-1957.
  The pastor of New Mexico : Peter Küppers's memoirs / translated, edited, and annotated by Tomas Jaehn.
     pages cm
  Includes bibliographical references.
  ISBN 978-1-63293-014-9 (softcover : alk. paper)
  1. Küppers, Peter, 1885-1957. 2. Catholic Church--New Mexico--Clergy--Biography. 3. New Mexico--Biography. I. Jaehn, Tomas, translator, editor, writer of added commentary. II. Jaehn, Tomas. Priest who made the schools bloom in the desert. III. Title.
  BX4705.K84A3 2014
  282.092--dc23
  [B]
                    2014024590

WWW.SUNSTONEPRESS.COM
SUNSTONE PRESS / POST OFFICE BOX 2321 / SANTA FE, NM 87504-2321 /USA
(505) 988-4418 / ORDERS ONLY (800) 243-5644 / FAX (505) 988-1025

To Pilar and Leah

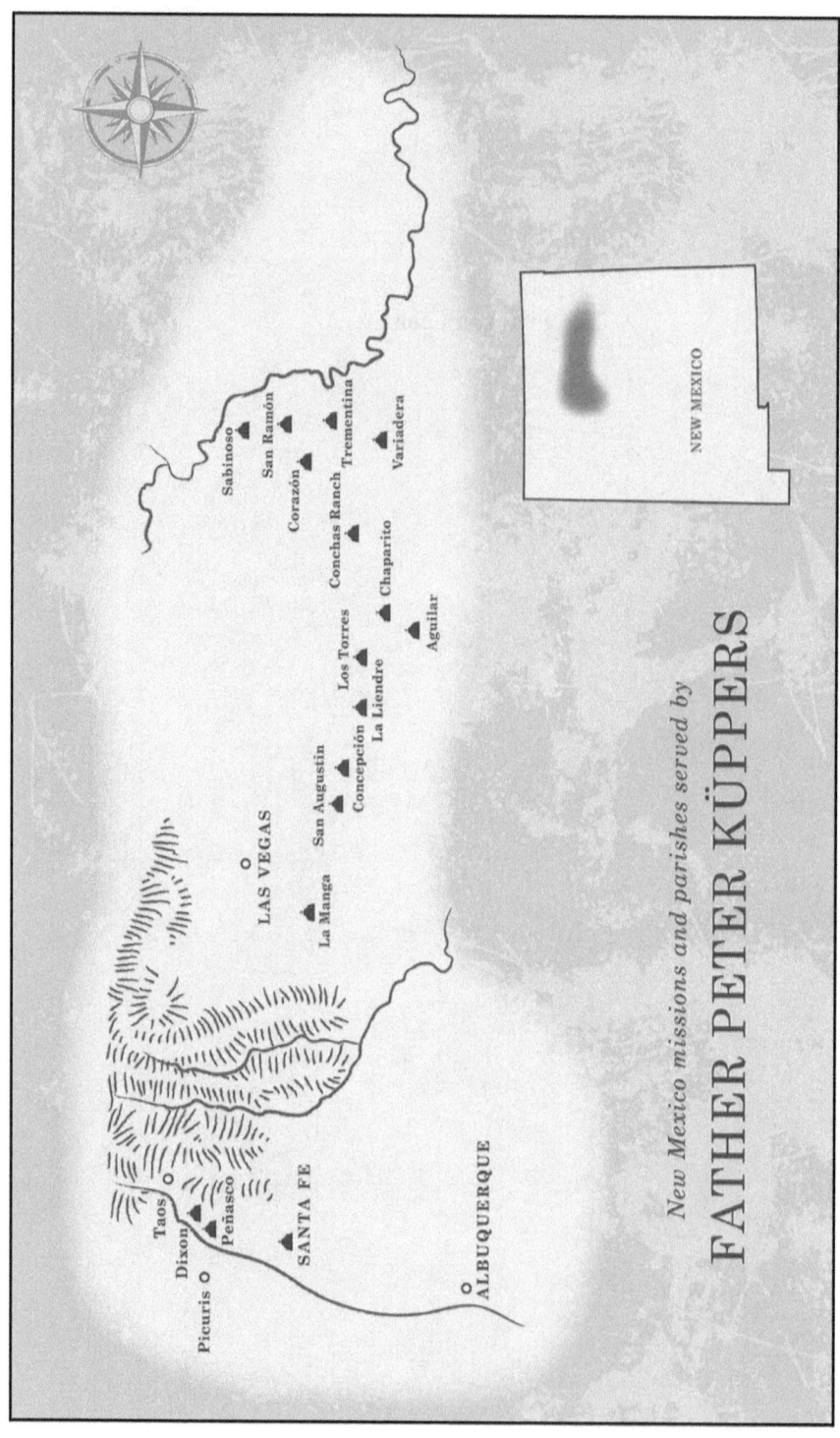

New Mexico Missions and Parishes served by Father Peter Küppers. Courtesy David Rohr, Santa Fe, New Mexico.

Contents

List of Illustrations	8
Preface	9
Archbishops of Santa Fe	16
A Little Boy	21
My Educational Years	31
To New Mexico	48
Life in Santa Fe, New Mexico	56
At the Cathedral	74
To Chaparito	94
"Soldiers of the Cross"	126
The Penitentes of Today	144
Rules and Admissions Regulations into the Morada	160
Appendix "The Priest Who Made the Schools Bloom in the Desert: Peter Küppers, 1911–1957"	169
Notes	181

List of Illustrations

Most Reverend John B. Pitaval / 16

Most Reverend Albert T. Daeger / 17

Most Reverend Rudolph A. Gerken / 18

Most Reverend Edwin V. Byrne / 19

Hubert Küppers / 22

Cathedral of Cologne, Germany / 45

New York City, New York / 50

Train Station, Lamy, New Mexico / 54

Monsignor Antoine Fourchegu / 57

St. Catherine's Indian School, Santa Fe, New Mexico / 59

Our Lady of Guadalupe Church, Santa Fe, New Mexico / 72

Church, Chaparito, New Mexico / 95

New Mexico Missions and Parishes served by Father Peter Küppers / 124

Peñasco, New Mexico / 141

Father Peter Küppers's original sketch of a *Pedernal* / 163

Father Peter Küppers's original sketch of symbols of Penitente membership / 163

Preface

The dream of "coming to America" was still alive for many Germans at the beginning of the 20th century. But often the vision was to be in vibrant urban centers like New York, Chicago, or San Francisco, or on fertile farmlands in Wisconsin or Texas, or at any of the fantasy-enticing landscapes across the wide-open spaces in the United States.

Peter Küppers was not necessarily an enthusiastic migrant but he liked the challenge to work overseas. As a priest, his dreams were to enter an established parish and play an important role in the advancement of the spiritual and social well-being of his flock, preferably in Texas. Hesitant due to personal circumstances, he initially turned down an offer to go to Texas only to end up in New Mexico. Küppers felt qualified for better and more important places. Besides, he had never heard of this place before and was accordingly disappointed, angry and somewhat arrogantly shaken in his own high self-esteem.

Peter Küppers was born in 1885, grew up in the western part of Germany near the Belgian border, undertook his theological studies at the University of Friborg in Switzerland, and was ordained at the grandest of grand cathedrals in Germany—the Cathedral of Cologne. Archbishop John B. Pitaval of the Archdiocese of Santa Fe then recruited him to come to New Mexico during a personal visit to Europe in 1911. Aside from one trip back to Germany in 1924 to visit his father and few short trips to Colorado and the mid-West, Küppers remained in New Mexico all his adult life. Yet he was not at all prepared for a life in the United States. His knowledge of the English language and American culture was rather limited. When he stepped first foot on American soil in New York, he got mad that folks in New York did not speak German. His initial contact with the American culture did not promise an easy transition into a life into New Mexico: he had no understanding at all of the Spanish language or the still predominant mores and traditions of the Hispanic and Native American populations.

Küppers's memoir, then, is his attempt to come to terms with his assignments in the Archdiocese of Santa Fe and with his life in general in northern New Mexico. His clerical life in New Mexico was by no means conflict-free. A stubborn Westfalian German, he collided with his various bosses, the Archbishops, over assignments; he conflicted with fellow priests over duties; and he initiated projects that were neither in the overall interest of the archdiocese nor approved—at times—by his superiors. For instance, struggling to find instructors for his rural schools, he hired unauthorized and non-English speaking nuns; he fought allegations of misuse of money, and he contended with rumors about having affairs with his housekeepers. His discords continued beyond the timeframe of his memoir, most notably with the "Dixon Case," which reached the New Mexico Supreme Court in the early 1950s and pertained to the financing of Catholic schools in Dixon through public moneys.

Küppers occasionally insinuated subtly at those disagreements, but often he explicitly rationalized that everything he did was in the best interest of the parish if not of the Archdiocese. And on those very rare occasions when he was at a loss of words, he pleaded simple misunderstandings. Still, his memoir shows that he seemed to have mastered life in this new and rather underdeveloped country reasonably well despite the occasional self-created roadblocks. Few original immigrant voices describe Northern New Mexico in the early twentieth century. Father Küppers's chronicle is indeed one of those few. He immersed himself into his new homeland and grew to know and to love Northern New Mexico and his Catholic and Hispanic population. Always biased, fierce, and protective of his flocks in Northern New Mexico, he became to some extent, what historian Ferenc Szasz once described as a "cultural broker," between local Hispanics and arriving Anglos. Küppers served the Archdiocese in Santa Fe at the Cathedral and the Guadalupe Church where he took his first wobbly steps in getting to know New Mexican culture, Catholic institutional customs, and the Spanish language.

A long stretch of service as a missionary priest in San Miguel County based out of Chaparito[1] followed. The contrast between densely populated German cities and towns (or Santa Fe, for that matter) and Chaparito could not have been any bigger. Wide open empty spaces, serving a population that only saw its priest once a month, a population that was still set in a barter society with little cash to support traveling priests, hours and hours of buggy or horseback rides between the various mission churches would have required adjustment from any priest, let alone one from Germany.

Eventually, after several years serving the ranchlands in Eastern San Miguel

County, Peter Küppers was assigned to the physically less strenuous parish of Peñasco and Dixon where he came into close contact with the Penitentes and in conflict, again, with clerical hierarchy in Santa Fe. Peñasco and Dixon were Küppers's final assignments in the Land of Enchantment. His struggles with fellow priests and staff at the Cathedral, not to mention his brief excommunication—likely for disobedience—took their toll. Toward the end of his life, Küppers built on his property, his own small chapel for spiritual guidance and tended to his orchards just off the road to Taos at the turnoff to Dixon. He died on March 23, 1957 in Colorado Springs.

While this memoir is a reflection of his life from earliest childhood in Germany to his work as a priest in New Mexico, Küppers's emphasis is on New Mexico and its people—on Santa Fe, Chaparito and San Miguel County, and Peñasco-Dixon. He likely maintained notes about his experiences (if they existed, they did not survive) and life in anticipation of writing this memoir. I would speculate that this memoir was written in the 1930s during his time in Peñasco and Dixon and thus might have coincided with a host of troubles that Küppers encountered in the late 1920s and 1930s. His quandaries included disagreements with Archbishop Rudolph A. Gerken, spats with fellow priests, accusations of affairs with his housekeepers, and allegations of monetary improprieties (not for personal gain but for the benefit of his parishes). The combination of these dilemmas led to a brief excommunication. Under those circumstances, perhaps his mood was reflected in parts of his memoir. His account is strangely separated into two distinct literary styles, which are difficult to explain, if at all, but might have been caused by Küppers's transforming dispositions at the time. A certain impatience to get this memoir complete can also be ascertained in the second part.

In the first half of his memoir covering his times in Germany, Santa Fe and Chaparito, Küppers is engaged in telling a story. He is entertaining, light-hearted, and at times humorous. As an indication of his personal character, he was certainly able to poke fun at himself. Written in the more personal and compelling 'I' format and sprinkling simple anecdotal stories into his account, Küppers loosely emulated the very popular late 19th and early 20th centuries Bavarian author Ludwig Thoma (1864–1921). Particularly Thoma's *Lausbuben Geschichten* (Rascals' stories) comes to mind when reading Küppers's stories. Küppers, of the right age for Thoma's folksy Bavarian tales, might have read them during his late teenage years when the tales were certainly trendy in Germany. Thoma was an expert in canvassing rural and small-town folks and their ways of life, pointing out their confinements, arrogance, and their occasional philistinism. In his mocking ways, he also took on the arbitrariness of the government and church. Küppers tries with less literary quality than Thoma and only mildly successful, to present life around him in such amusingly packaged, sometimes satirical ways.

But Küppers did not by any means mock New Mexicans—quite to the contrary. He was very fond of the Hispanic New Mexicans (as long as they were good Catholics) and their culture, but the application of sarcasm, the rural and small town similarities, the set-up of stories, and the choice of words is reminiscent of Ludwig Thoma and makes Küppers often the typical German: slightly arrogant with a touch of priestly paternalism.

The second half of his account is quite different in tone and style. Küppers switches from his 'I' format into 3rd person, and turns from an animated storyteller into a distant, pseudo-objective observer of the events in Northern New Mexico. He loses the narrative autobiographical thread and instead weaves his life in Peñasco and Dixon around the story of the Penitentes.

The Hermandad de Nuestro Senior Jesus Nazareno as this centuries-old confraternity is officially called, has an uncertain origin. Some historians see the brotherhood as a uniquely New Mexican organization while others trace its origin back to Franciscan influence in Spain. Regardless of origin, as settlers inhabited isolated areas in the high country of Northern New Mexico, cut off from civilization, their Catholic religion took on ceremonies that were inappropriate in the eyes of the Catholic Church. Frequent conflicts arose between the Catholic Church and the Hermanos as some of their religious observations were carried on outside the strict supervision of the Roman Catholic Church and sometimes under intolerant parish priests, which exacerbated the clashes.

The Penitentes have unfortunately been known and today still remembered mostly for their self-flagellation but also for their melancholic hymns and their Holy Week rituals. In the mid 19th century, a young Franz Hunning, for instance, went 'penitentes hunting' to observe this bloody event, and so did boys in the 1930s when going "out there at night and hid behind the sage and cedars to watch them [. . .] drag their great crosses up a long, sloping cleared space" as Taos socialite Mable Dodge Luhan remembered. Still today, there is interest in investigating these practices. Less known was the brothers' devotion to their communities where they helped take care of the sick, the widowed, and those poor and down on their luck. Until 1947 when Archbishop Edwin V. Byrne offered the blessing and protection of the Catholic Church, the Penitentes and the parish priests had to come to an understanding. Peter Küppers seemed sympathetic toward the Penitentes' situation as long as they put the Church's ceremonies before their duties to the Morada, their own house of worship.

Küppers quotes excessively from the Most Reverend John Baptist Salpointe's *Soldiers of the Cross*, about the Penitentes' lives in Northern New Mexico. But he quotes from Salpointe's for other purposes as well. *Soldiers of the Cross* is an account of early activities of the missionaries in the Southwest, a hardy group, with whom Küppers could associate and to which Küppers undoubtedly felt he belonged to— even decades later. Küppers who was fond of Archbishop Salpointe and his work, often felt that the conditions these pioneer missionaries found themselves in and the struggles they endured to establish the foundations for the Catholic Church in the Southwest applied in a narrower sense to his own missionary work in Northern New Mexico two decades later. After all, he still made house calls on horseback or with a buggy (day or night) and he built chapels and schoolhouses with his bare hands with little help from the locals.

Peter Küppers's memoir is a typed manuscript held in the archives of the Archdiocese of Santa Fe's Historic/Artistic Patrimony, Archives and Museum. Küppers intended to publish his memoir in book form (he contemplated New York publisher Alfred A. Knopf) but for unexplained reasons this did not happen. Instead he published modified segments of his memoir in a serialized version in a German social science journal in St. Louis. As publications go, it was a clean error-free chronicle of his life.

His typed manuscript was far less error-free. Küppers was a well-educated person who finished his humanistic schooling with a Gymnasium diploma and a graduate university degree and had knowledge in German, French and Latin—this is to say that although he may not have been the most gifted writer or novelist, he knew German grammar and orthography. Still, his manuscript, at times, suggests otherwise and leads me to believe that it was truly a first, perhaps a second draft. In order to make this manuscript readable and turn it into a publishable piece of writing, it required editorial decisions from the outset.

There were, for instance, two draft versions of the manuscript. Both renderings were very similar in context, but at times slightly differed. Occasionally Küppers arranged the paragraphs a bit different, and once or twice, he left stories incomplete in one of the drafts. In instances like that, the other draft had to be consulted to understand what he was saying. One draft, however, that was most complete I chose as the "official" draft version. With regard to translating Küppers's story it did not matter much—both versions despite all their small differences are telling the same story.

Some of the manuscript chapters had titles, while others did not. Where titles were missing, I created them. Küppers, in the available drafts, had no concept of the need for paragraphs or their proper placement when he occasionally used them. Often he merged several thoughts into pages. I split them into paragraphs for easier reading or redirected paragraphs to where they made more sense. Occasionally, he is off in his days and months and timelines. Since they had no bearing on the story itself and I had no means to verify dates, I did not correct those mistakes.

Especially during the first part of his memoir, Küppers, in an attempt to be jovial and engaging, often applied direct speech, but frequently neglected to use quotation marks and/or indents to indicate the direct speech. I added quotation marks and indents when applicable.

Küppers's draft itself presented challenges for a translation into English as well. His (obviously manual) typewriter did not have keys for the German Umlaute (ä-ö-ü) and he often failed to use the conventional substitutions (ae-oe-ue), instead just using a-o-u. However, the two dots over consonants in a German conjugated verb often represent the conjunctive or future version of it. Not having the Umlaute made it at times challenging to determine if Küppers did something or just wanted to do it or had plans to it in the future. Still, the context of his stories nearly always provided the clue if something in fact did happen or not. Similar problems occurred with nouns but those potential misunderstandings were easily detected in the context. For instance, *Kuchen* means cake, but *Küchen* indicates kitchens or *Gute* means good, but *Güte* means kindness.

Errors, if one can call them that, also happened sporadically in what linguists call "code switching." Küppers inadvertently used an English language word instead of the German word. Occasionally his German grammar was faulty and sometimes he used a German word with the wrong meaning. All these are signs that Küppers was becoming immersed into life in New Mexico—linguistically and otherwise. He did not adopt, however, the somewhat laid-back American manners with regard to titles and salutations—there he remained very German: it was, and still is to some extent, conventional in the German language to address Küppers as, for instance "Mister Pastor Küppers." To provide better flow of the story and to adhere to English conventions, I used this German convention of "Herr" or "Frau" in front of occupational titles sparingly.

Typographical and grammatical errors, which were plentiful in the manuscript are irrelevant to a translation and disappeared in the conversion into English. The same is correct for other translation-related concerns: no attempts have been made to reproduce antiquated German forms and the occasional regional dialect that found its way into his memoir. Since Küppers used occasionally parentheses in his text, I used brackets to distinguish my comments from his.

Küppers also wasn't very well versed in punctuation rules or did not feel like observing such rules at that point of his drafts. Subsequently, some of his long, long sentences had to be closely interpreted to find the correct meaning and best possible English translation.

Father Küppers appeared absent-minded at times during his writing sessions and sometimes one had to read segments of stories several time to figure out their meanings. On a few rare occasions Küppers was truly absent minded and began to write down his thoughts only to switch in-mid story to a new train of thought that appeared important to him, only to pick up the original story a few pages later without even a hint of another introduction. In those rare cases, I moved paragraphs to the appropriate place to support the flow of reading. As with every task of translating a text from one language into another, there is room for interpretation but I tried to stay as close to Peter Küppers's character, word choices, and meaning as possible.

The goal of this translation, after all, is to give the reader the opportunity to read a story. The story of an immigrant to Northern New Mexico who had no clue about where New Mexico was and who knew very little English and no Spanish at all. It was a story that Father Peter Küppers felt was worth telling. And with this story he allows readers a glimpse into the worries and hardships and also the successes and pleasures of an immigrant in a strange land. With it, he also provides readers a sense of rural and Catholic life in Northern New Mexico during the first half of the twentieth century.

In 1997, years before I considered working on a translation of Peter Küppers's memoirs, I gave a paper in honor of the Archdiocese of Santa Fe's 400th anniversary on one aspect of Father Küppers's life—his struggles to build schools and to educate children. This paper was subsequently published in the late Father Tom Steele's anthology *Seeds of Struggle, Harvest of Faith*. With gracious permission from the publishers Paul Rhetts and Barb Anwalt, this paper "The Priest Who Made Schools Bloom in the Desert: Peter Küppers, 1911–1957" is reproduced in the appendix. The footnotes pertaining to Father Küppers's memoir in the article refer to the original German version and not to the English translation and are therefore not applicable to the published translation in this book. Since biographical information for the article was derived from his memoirs, it is therefore at times repetitive. Still, the article will provide additional information about Peter Küppers's life in New Mexico.

—Tomas Jaehn
Santa Fe, New Mexico

The Four Archbishops of Santa Fe under whom Peter Küppers served

Most Reverend John B. Pitaval, D.D., 5th Archbishop of Santa Fe from 1909–1918. Courtesy Palace of the Governors Photo Archives (NMHM/DCA), #65112.

Most Reverend Albert T. Daeger, O.F.M; D.D., 6th Archbishop of Santa Fe from 1919–1932.
Courtesy Palace of the Governors Photo Archives (NMHM/DCA), #50375.

Most Reverend Rudolph A. Gerken, D.D., 7th Archbishop of Santa Fe from 1933–1943. Courtesy Palace of the Governors Photo Archives (NMHM/DCA), #50386.

Most Reverend Edwin V. Byrne, D.D., 8th Archbishop of Santa Fe from 1943–1963. Courtesy Palace of the Governors Photo Archives (NMHM/DCA), #65115.

A Little Boy

Had someone told me on 25 June 1885, the day I entered this world that I will one day end up a priest in New Mexico I would have thoroughly mocked that person. But, as far as I can remember, nobody but my dear mother was nearby and so I just screamed instead, although I am not quite sure of that either. I believe, however, she comforted me by whispering some nice words into my ear. So many years passed since then, that I do not remember these minor details.

As the years went on, more and more little brothers and sisters appeared. As I developed more common sense, I noticed that a woman came to the house from time to time always holding a little basket. And every time she said "You have another little brother or sister, and I brought it home to your Mama." I once asked her "where are these little brothers and sisters coming from? Are you buying them?"

"No," she responded, "your Papa is doing the buying, I only deliver all those he bought." "Just make sure he doesn't buy too many," I advised her in all my wisdom. She simply laughed, but today I know that my Papa bought fourteen in all and I was the first one.

I was about five years old when once again a basket was delivered to the house. Now I had a serious talk with my dear Papa and took him to task. Addressing him the way my Mama did, I said: "Papa Hubert, you seem to have a lot of money to buy so many brothers and sisters. How much did you pay for me?"

First, he scolded me because I called him Hubert. But when I looked so sad, he stroked my curly hair and said: "You are my dearest because you are the first one God sold me. But I did not have to pay anything for you because I did not have much cash then." I looked at my father with big eyes and told him what many people had to say about cheap items: "That's quite cheap, but what's cheap, isn't worth much."

Hubert Küppers, Peter Küppers's father at age 90 in 1947. He died in 1948. Courtesy the Author.

He looked at me in his serious way and slowly said, "Didn't you understand what I just told you? The good Lord sent you. I was waiting for you and when you arrived, I said 'My darling baby came directly from God, and you will return to him later on.'" Yet, I thought "No, I'd rather stay with Papa and Mama who love me just as much as the dear Lord."

It was about a year later or perhaps even the same year—my memory is a bit shaky because of old age—that my sweet mother took me to church one afternoon. I understood fairly well already how to pray. Suddenly my mother whispered to me: "Do you know who lives in this church?" After having looked around in the church, I said: "There isn't anybody here, but you told me often enough that God lives here. I have never seen him here, though."

She explained the concept to me, but I only understood that this same God, who gave me to my father and mother, would like to have me back, eventually. I didn't like this idea at all and threw such a tantrum, that my mother left the church with me in a hurry. For the longest time, there was quite a bit of commotion and uproar when I went to church with my mother. Finally, as it happens with everything, I got used to it.

My sweet mother once told me about the day I was very sick, when my brother Joseph—while playing—hit me with a piece of wood over the head and everybody thought I was dead. After I regained consciousness I couldn't remember any of the silly things I said, but my mother told me that everybody was laughing about me. That is everybody, but father and mother who were very concerned. The accident may have resulted in some permanent damage because in later years, I haven't always made the wisest of choices.

Still, mother once said: "If he survives and has potential to become a good pastor, then I would love for him to attend a university." I think that was the reason why I had to begin studying at such early age and it sure wasn't easy. I thought my first teacher knew far less that I did. But I was wrong and he proved it one day by simply putting me over his knee. The spanking itself wasn't so bad, but the throbbing that followed was a different story.

As I grew older, became more careful, and developed more smarts, another thing happened to me: One day, when I was once again in trouble, I smugly filled the seat of my pants with wool I had previously commandeered after my father sheared a sheep. Now I thought: "It won't hurt so much anymore when I have to step forward." The taller I grew, the harder it was for the teacher to put me over his knee. Instead, I had to step forward and on command "hands to toes" bend over to present the tight seat of my pants to receive the usual penalty with a paddle. Afterwards it was difficult to sit quietly on the hard wooden school benches.

On this day the teacher, however, outsmarted me. When he noticed that something just wasn't quite right, he reached into my pants and pulled out what was in it, namely the sheep wool. The consequence can be easily imagined. I was now convinced that the teacher was smarter than I, and from then on I had respect for him. Consequently, I became much more patient and tolerant, especially since my good father kept that piece of wool as a reminder and whenever I was in danger of pulling another stunt he immediately showed me the piece. It turned out that the teacher and my father were in cahoots.

One day, when I was still a little boy, my father called me into his shop and asked, "Well, my son, what would you like to be when you grow up?"
"I would like to become a pastor," I replied readily. I could tell my father was very happy with this response. Later, when he told my mother, she looked at me with pride, and I decided for sure to become a pastor. From that point on, school went easier and the teacher treated me nicer, even with a certain respect.

My father was from a good home and so was my mother. When my father married my mother—I don't remember it but he told me about it later—he had already bought his own house. But the wedding almost did not happen. As a dashing soldier serving in the military at the time, his entire unit was ordered to take a bath in the Rhine River. Although he was an excellent swimmer, he almost drowned on this occasion had a fellow soldier not pulled him out. When my father mentioned this story for the first time, I told him: "Had you drowned I would not have had the chance to become a priest." What he thought about this, I don't know. In any event, he did not drown and I became a priest.

To become a priest I had to learn how to pray. Although I already knew my morning and evening prayers, I still had to learn the rosary. I was smart enough that learning it was fairly easy but it was quite lengthy and sometimes boring. In the winter, after supper my family always recited the rosary and all the journeymen and apprentices employed in my father's carpentry shop were required to attend. Otherwise, they risked being fired the next morning. My father always acted on the principle of "Good worshipers, good laborers" and "poor worshipers, lazy laborers." These principles were generally true, even though nowadays not much time is spent praying anymore. Therefore, I had to recite the rosary.

Everything went fine except when I felt that ten "Ave Maria" were too many and skipped a few. One evening, my father must have been especially attentive, and he was good in counting, because that evening I left out two or three "Ave Maria" and finished the rosary too quickly. I had to pray a few additional ones, and this time on my knees and all by myself. From this experience I derived the first logical conclusion in my life: it pays to be honest, especially with the Lord.

I always made sure to have excitement in life, even when it meant now and then to get the raw end of a deal—be it by happenstance or through my own stupidity. My dear mother spoiled me a little too much and when I used to come home from school in the afternoons and did not want to exchange my shoes for the rural clogs, she commented calmly: "There is something in him. He surely will end up a pastor."

My father took a practical approach to steer this professional desire in the right direction. Early on, he sent me to a teacher who taught Latin to small children. He was clever and knew more Latin than my school teacher. But I just could not comprehend then, why I had to learn so much Latin—particularly, since our priest never spoke it with us. Only in church and then only with the Lord did he converse in Latin, and then it was the Sexton who often answered. Quite often the answer came back really loud and I thought the Sexton might have been angry. I was too young to really comprehend Latin. The Latin teacher spanked me hard and often enough, that I finally had it with this Latin business, at least as far as my bottom was concerned, and instead of attending my private language lessons I skipped them once in a while. To be sure, I always prepared a good excuse for missing my lessons. Eventually the teacher did not believe my excuses anymore even though I had the kindness and forbearance to personally deliver my apologies. To this day, I believe my father joined forces with him in this matter because when I arrived for class after having again missed one, the teacher gave me a beating I never forgot. I was convinced that he had no right to treat me that way and thought: "One of these days I'll get you for that."

Now, whenever skipping private lessons again, I was smart enough not to apologize in person but rather to write the teacher notes. These notes in which I replicated my father's handwriting as best I could, I slipped under the door of his apartment at opportune times. He must have found each of my notes because he continued to be quite friendly for several weeks afterward. He was always very polite and keenly interested in my apologies. I was certain he was suddenly so cordial only because he had to respect—what I thought, he thought—were my father's writings. I knew that the teacher respected what my father had to say in these notes, and so I continued to eagerly create absentee notes.

One Saturday evening, then, the teacher paid a visit to my father's house. I didn't feel too well and this indisposition increased the longer the two men stayed in my father's study. Had my father not been home, this little indisposition would not have bothered me at all. But I felt increasingly worse, that even my mama noticed and asked attentively whether I had eaten some bad food. When I saw the love in her eyes, I ruefully admitted my crimes. She nodded understandingly and asked: "How about taking Latin classes with our priest. He knows the language much better and you do like him." The priest appreciated me and I was not afraid of him because he was very good to all the children. It should be noted here that it was Father Hoegel, next to my mother, who I have to thank for taking up the priesthood.

The discussion between my father and the teacher was still going on. I felt a little better, when my mother finally went to see them. After she finally returned, she comforted me and talked me into returning with her to see my father and the teacher. Holding on to my mother's apron, I had to go into the study. The teacher looked pretty annoyed, even after I bowed politely. To my surprise, my father was very sweet and I think he did not want his oldest son to learn Latin with methods that include the cane which the teacher used on me occasionally. Finally I had my way, but my father taught me a lesson: "honesty is the best policy." I understood that easily. But I made my point that I was not going to return to that teacher nor would I want to learn any Latin from him. The teacher was very quiet. My father understood the situation clearly and decided to have a talk with our priest. But he reminded me: "If you don't improve, you will not become a priest." At that point I decided seriously to learn Latin from our priest. The teacher never spoke another word with me, but later my father told me: "Thrashing has its place, but with thrashing alone one cannot learn Latin."

Why I liked the priest so much is easily explained. He came twice a week to school to teach religion and was good, but firm, with children. Although being a little hard of hearing, we all loved him. He was the one who prepared me for my first confession. Because he was hard of hearing we had to go to the sacristy for confession. Like all others, I was shaking with the expectation of things to come. I remember that he was very supportive and when I got stuck because of excitement and fear, he pretended not to have noticed. I was afraid he might not give me absolution. Yet after I was through telling my sins, many of which I read off a piece of paper in order to not forget any, he told me affectionately through the little window of the confessional: "You have been a good boy." He did not deny me absolution, and asked me to remain a good boy so that I would become a good pastor. I think the good Father was smiling when he said that. Thereafter, I left the confessional, quickly prayed my penance, left the church, performed several somersaults, and ran home. At home, still excited, I related everything to my father and mother, including the sins. After that I was always good to the pastor.

But I digress, the day following this memorable Saturday evening discussion between my father and the Latin teacher, my father went to see the good priest and I returned to my Latin lessons but this time with the priest. I think my former teacher was annoyed about that. I have never lost a war, even though I may have occasionally lost a battle.

I will never forget how nice the good Father talked to me and how he explained everything about how to become a priest. I was the star student and I had a swell time. Mother purchased a pair of velvet slippers for me and after I came home from school, I was allowed to use them for my Latin lessons. All my friends envied me. I had so much fun going to see the priest that I went almost daily. I had one concern, though. I could not picture myself becoming a Sexton. The current Sexton was a good man but I was afraid of him and I knew he did not like me. Unfamiliar with the proper process, I thought before becoming a priest I had to become a Sexton, and that would have cost him his job.

There were others in the presbytery who liked me: Old Mrs. Moll and her daughter Barbara. Why these two were so nice to me is still today a mystery to me. I believe it was because my father raised lots of chickens, and on occasions I took a fat one over to them and as talkative as I was, I always reported the latest gossip. As far as I was concerned, I knew why I liked them. Every time I came to see them, there was a treat waiting for me: a piece of cake or flan, and other sweets. My parents were pleased to see me going to the presbytery after school. They knew I was well taken care of and stayed out of trouble. I never again missed a Latin lesson, studied hard, and pleased the good Father. We remained good friends and may God praise him, Mrs. Moll and Barbara.

At home, my father ran a busy shop and, therefore, could not regularly attend mass. But my mother went every morning and I had to join her every time. We employed a maid, who also liked me, and when mother and I went to church, she took care of the housework.

One Sunday, our maid, who was a relative of mine, left early in the morning by train after mass to attend some festivity. She promised to have a present for me tonight upon her return. Why I didn't tell my parents about that, I don't know. So that evening I walked to the train station, a half hour away, to wait for her arrival. But she just did not come. The night was dark, pitch black to be exact, and I was so afraid to walk the country road back home that I stayed at the train station until midnight when finally a train arrived and she stepped off. She looked surprised. There was a man accompanying her who I hadn't seen before and I felt awkward because I didn't understand what he was doing there. But I was glad that she was back and we started to walk home. The walk home wasn't far and she was talking uneasily about my father and mother. The man with her kept grumbling but I didn't know why, since I did not know him.

Suddenly a bicycle came toward us and a man jumped off when he saw us. I recognized him immediately, it was my father. He carried a whip which I knew all too well. Never before had I made such a rotten acquaintance with the whip, probably because I stayed out so long. On top of the beating I had to ride home standing behind him on the bicycle [axle]. When my mother saw me, she started crying but was happy to have her boy back. When the maid did not come to work the next day, I sneaked out of the house to find her. I found her at her mother's place, and learned she did not want to return to us. I was screaming and screaming until she agreed to take me home—and to stay with us. The initial defeat turned into victory.

The time for my first Holy Communion came. Although I was not quite old enough yet, the good Father eagerly accepted me: "He is intelligent enough and will soon start his secondary education." Preparations for the Holy Communion took almost a year. I always attended classes, but almost ruined my communion by nearly losing the good Father's favor.

I had a friend who was not quite as pious as I. Every Sunday afternoon we all had to attend services as well as bible studies prior to the service. The church was usually crowded. That particular Sunday my friend mentioned that my uncle had beautiful ripe peaches and apricots in his garden and we agreed to pick a few before church. The peaches, however, were particularly delicious and we missed the sound of the church bells. When we were about to leave the orchard, Uncle Alois showed up. We took off as fast as we could and although we heard him screaming behind us, he could not catch us. How my father and mother knew about it almost instantly, I could not understand.

As every Sunday after the service, the entire family met for a bite to eat. Despite having skipped service, I arranged to be at the gathering in time. I wasn't very hungry, although the cake looked, as always, very inviting. My father was seemingly nice to me, while my mother was so quiet and withdrawn that I followed her example. My father offered me a big piece of cake, but I still felt the peaches in my stomach. When I couldn't manage to eat the piece of cake, my father made small talk, asking if the priest asked me about the catechism.

"The good Pastor does that all the time," I try to divert. "What did he ask you," my father kept inquiring and I described the answers I gave the priest. My father immediately took me to see the priest. I don't remember how the situation ended but the following Sunday I redeemed myself and regained the good Father's love and respect.

It was again bible study time at church and as always a lot of adults were present. We children stood in rows of two along the church benches so that the priest could walk between us. As mentioned earlier, he was hard of hearing. He asked: "What are the signs of God's true church?" and pointed to my friend, who stole the peaches with me that Sunday, to answer. He paused and then answered: "Honor your father and your mother that you may live long on earth" and added a few additional phrases so that the answer appeared long enough. To my surprise, and I think, to the surprise of the entire congregation, the priest replied: "Very good, my son." Some people started laughing and the priest turned around looking confused. This was too much for me, because the given answer was obviously false, and with a strong voice, I shouted that this was not the correct answer, and quickly rattled off the proper answer. The priest reconsidered and agreed with me. After the service, some bullies waited for me outside and beat me up. Back at home, however, I received an oversize piece of cake as a reward for my behavior in church. The next day I went proudly to the presbytery with my Latin grammar and text book in my arm, I even took my slippers.

There was one time, though, where I was really off in my judgment. It was on a Sunday, at a lake near the village, called Titepolke—and I don't know why it had that name. Our head teacher always advised us not to swim in it, even though it wasn't deep enough to drown. So, many of my friends went there occasionally to take a bath and to cool off. One Sunday, it was very hot, my friends convinced me that I had to learn to swim at some point and so I came along. We changed clothes in a nearby cornfield and jumped into the water. I had so much fun, that I jumped repeatedly into and out of the water. When I was just about to jump into the water once again, I saw a man running like crazy through the fields. It was our head teacher. I had barely enough time to grab my clothes and run off. I ran and ran—how far I don't remember, but when I finally stopped to get dressed, I noticed that I had lost my shoes. I couldn't find my socks either. Consequently, I was forced to walk home barefoot, which was a whole lot better than the fate of some of my comrades, who were caught by the teacher—or so I thought. When I came home, my father gave me a whipping. The following day I received an encore from my teacher. So, in the final analysis I was worse off and I never forgot that.

Every fall on Sundays, we boys got together to go rabbit hunting. One Sunday we changed our plans and decided to go for some honey out of a neighbor's bee hives. But concerned with the potential repercussions, I chickened out and secretly sneaked back home. My conscience was clean, but I can't describe the surprise when on Monday after school, I saw that beekeeper at our house. I was immediately put on the spot when he accused me of having stolen his honey. That was too much for me and I became rude. The neighbor even went so far as to request to see and smell my Sunday suit. After the inquisition was over and I was found innocent, I could finally eat lunch. As revenge, however, I walked by the neighbor's house that same evening and threw a stone at his window.

The next time in confession I professed my misdeed to the good pastor who had a smile running across his face, when I told the story. Still, he ordered me to come clean with my father, so that he could pay for the window. When I replied that this would be inconceivable because a heavy whipping would be the consequence, he understood: "So that nobody will find out who broke the window, I will pay for it," and added, that if I wanted to become a priest, I had to stop breaking windows. That was a reasonable request and I never again took revenge. For his favor, I was always indebted to the priest. In later years, as a student of theology I reminded the priest of this story to which he responded: "You were not always an innocent boy."

In spring I made my first Holy Communion. It was a grand day for me. I was well prepared and my best prayer was about my desire to become a priest that I eventually became. On communion day, my mother prepared the very best lunch I had ever tasted. All my relatives were invited. I felt very important and that evening my parents and I tried to figure out how long my theological education might take. My father figured: "This will not take much longer, the years will pass by quickly."

In the fall, real life began. I was sent to a bigger school with a much more complex and structured curriculum. It was a boarding school [near the border town of Sittard in Holland]. I would have preferred a regular high school, but my opinion was not asked. The priest had already arranged everything. On the first Sunday in September, taking almost all day, I said good bye to all my relatives and friends. When I finally returned home that evening and found my mother in tears, it hit me that from now on I was going to be on my own, without my dear mother nearby. I started to cry, too. After she kissed and hugged me, I went to bed sadly. I will never forget that moment. My father did not cry, at least I did not see any tears but he was very quiet and did not say a word. In the morning I got up very early, and I cried bitterly when I bade farewell to my mother. My father accompanied me to my new school which took almost all day by train. On this memorable morning I saw the dearest person who ever appeared in my life for the last time alive. But I knew that she was watching over me from far above and whenever I looked at her picture, I knew I was always going to love her, because she was my very dear mother.

The book is dedicated to my dear mother and my dear father.

My Educational Years

By the time I was twelve years old, the best time of my life had passed. I was in school for about six months when one Sunday morning my uncle appeared at the school. It was after mass and all the students were in the assembly hall, when the principal called for me. To be called to the director was generally not a good sign and I nearly blacked out, but made it to his office after all. He looked at me with sad eyes, took my hand, and told me that my uncle was here to take me home. I was granted a leave of three days because my mother was very sick. I had tears in my eyes, and it turned worse when my uncle told me bluntly that my mother had died. We took the train home together. Yes, the dearest person I have ever had in this world was dead. I did not have a mother anymore.

Three days later was the funeral and afterwards I had to be carried home from the cemetery. The same evening my father suggested that it would be better that I returned to school tomorrow and that he would take me there. I did not want him to take me, because I knew how difficult it was for him to leave the house at this point. The next morning he took me to the train, but although my grief was deep, I did not cry. The train had barely left the station my tears were running and when I had to switch trains at another station I decided not to continue but to buy a return ticket home instead. I took the next train back and did not cry once until I reach home. The maid, who was the first one to see me, looked at me as if I were a person from another planet. Then she screamed for my father who was in his carpenter shop. All he said was that if I stayed I had to work and learn the business. "It might be for the better anyway if you do not become a priest," he added.

Behind the church was a small chapel displaying the crucifix scene. In the evening, my father invited me to go with him to this chapel where he then asked me if I really did not want to return to school. I have never forgotten this, just as I have never forgotten the last time I saw my mother at the funeral. I will also always remember that the good old priest told me how very happy and content my mother looked shortly before her death, when she saw my first report card. I never caused my dear mother any grief and it was she who told me that night in the chapel to become a priest. The next day I left alone for school.

For Easter, students were not allowed to take a vacation, but I received permission to go home. Why, I could never figure out, but when it was time to leave for summer vacation, the principal sweet-talked me into staying. I think that my father had been in cahoots with the principal in this matter.

One Sunday, shortly after the first anniversary of my mother's death I had a visitor. I ran into the visitors' room to find my father waiting for me accompanied by a well-dressed lady. I looked at her with big eyes and asked "who is she?"

My father smiled sadly and asked quietly: "Wouldn't you like to have a new mother?"

"Bah," I said, "is it going that fast?" Then I had to shake hands with her. Later I thought that having a mother would be good during the summer break. However, while home during the next summer vacation, a big fight ensued in the family.

I generally went to mass every morning. However one morning, a school friend who wasn't quite as devout as I was, visited and talked me into trading mass for a walk. Upon our return from this stroll my father made a big fuss. I blamed my stepmother for it who was not at fault at all. It was the two of us alone who were at fault here. As far as I remember, my father sent me back to school early where I had to confess the reasons for my shortened vacation.

At school, only two other students were there who had not left for vacation. Together we did not have much to do, were bored and came up with quite a few tricks. In the schoolyard stood a lone apple tree and the fruits were a great temptation for us. Just like Adam and Eve in paradise, we were not allowed to eat the apples. But, just like with our ancestors, temptation prevailed. Since most teachers and professors were gone on vacation, we found ample opportunities to go after the apples. So, once dusk was approaching, we quickly climbed the tree, and within five minutes the sin was done. Any regrets we might have had came too late, as one teacher saw us from his window. Whether he saw all of us or just me, I don't know, but I was the only one who was ordered to see him in his room. To my surprise he knew more than I did.

Six years of boarding school went by fast. We had to study hard, and vacations were always a great relief. I liked to go home but always made sure that the report cards turned out well. Otherwise, I would not have been allowed to come home. I remember two things from my vacations: my father never allowed me to smoke or to drink, not even a glass of beer. Only on Sundays did he bring home a liter of beer for the entire family, after having spent a couple of hours after dinner for business reasons in the local tavern with all the other honoraries. My father was well respected in the community.

There were always apprentices in my father's shop, and one evening, I went with two of them for a walk to smoke my first cigar. Luckily, my father wasn't home when I returned so I went straight to bed.

One Saturday afternoon my father was out again, and another apprentice and I went to see my father's cave-like cellar which was underneath the kitchen. The apprentice—Paul was his name—and I were good friends, and when he suggested we go and get a bottle of wine I eagerly agreed. I knew that this was the place my father kept his wine and so did Paul, an orphan who was taken in by my father. Next to the locked door to the cellar was a hole in the wall for fresh air. This hole was just big enough for us to crawl through. Since the hole in the wall was somewhat high off the floor, I fell into the cellar—head first. I took a bottle and wanted to leave the way I came in, but I was too short and could not reach the hole in the wall. The temptation to try the wine was great, and while my friend stood watch outside, I pulled the cork out of the bottle and took a sip. Then I tried again to reach the opening, but to no avail. I took a second sip from the bottle yet was not able to leave the basement. Shortly thereafter, I felt like Noah after the great flood: the wine went to my head and, I think, into my legs, too, because they felt so awfully heavy. I had no idea what was going on in the outside world and did not make it to dinner. Everything came to light when my step-mother happened to enter the cellar and to her great surprise found me. The bottle was also found. When I appeared in front of my father, instead of giving me the well-deserved whipping, he gave me a lecture I never forgot. There was no reason to turn in my friend, since he didn't taste any of the wine.

If one is too confident in a student, that student himself will be over-confident, and if one gives him too much freedom, he will expect that freedom. Although life at the boarding school was hard, today I am thankful for it. We had good food, studied proficiently, but also had to do tasks not many students now-a-days would agree to do. We cleaned classrooms, sleeping rooms, and dishes after meals. We had three dormitory rooms, separated according to age, and even during the coldest winter there were always windows open. There was no running water, only a wash table in the corner where twenty-five students took a sponge bath. Every day we had to fill up large containers with water, so that we could open the faucets and wash up.

During winter season the water was often frozen and we had to crush the ice. Once a week the "locus" [Latin; nick name for toilettes] had to be cleaned and we students were the ones who had to do that. Since there were no bathtubs, twice a week we made the twenty minute trip on foot to the river where we had a hidden bathing spot. We used that spot well into the winter. When it became really cold, we dropped our clothes quickly in the nearby bushes, jumped for very brief moments into the ice cold water, got back out, dressed, and ran home. When we arrived at the school we were fresh and warm. Illness was almost unknown at school. For entertainment we played handball [European team sport] and soccer, and more than once I left the field with bruises all over my body. Bowling and other games were also part of our off-time entertainment.

Course work was very demanding; the daily curriculum covered Latin, Greek, Mathematics, German, French, and many other subjects. Those who completed school were certainly not dumb. The time before the semi-annual exams was the hardest. There was no time for entertainment, and even during time of relaxation we hit the books. During our bi-weekly strolls we walked in groups of three or four and studied. The pressure was on because failing an exam meant repeating an entire year. And we almost failed one of them. It was during the last exam while working hard for our final diploma. Our Greek language professor did not like some of my classmates. He was a devout and good-natured priest whose patience we more than once abused.

A few weeks before the final exams he did, indeed, lose his patience with us. One of the students had a very good and high-quality camera, which he set up in the classroom while the professor was writing on the blackboard. When we all laughed, the teacher turned abruptly around, and the student pushed the button of the camera. The professor was so startled that he forgot to confiscate the plate and we developed a wonderful snapshot of him. That the camera was lost didn't bother us so much. His threat that he will take his revenge in the final exam, however, concerned us mightily. And the headache became bigger as the day of the exam came closer.

The day before the exam, out of desperation, we developed a smart plan to seek encouragement. Instead of going for our usual walk, twelve of us separated from the rest of the students and went to Sittard a small town about twenty minutes away. We all had some money to go to an inn. After one, two, three mugs of beer for thirsty throats, one could see desperate students spread out around the pool tables.

We forgot the world around us and no grief or anxiety could bother us until one of the students screamed: "The professor is coming." The result was desperation.

"Don't run, keep playing," I bellowed, when the professor entered the inn with a "Good day, Gentlemen."

We answer with a whispering "Good day, Herr Professor."

It was the professor, Dr. Alois, our theology teacher whose exam was first on the list. He sat down at a table, ordered a mug of beer while nervously we tried to continue the game of pool. Nobody spoke a word. When the professor finished his beer, he got up, said good-bye, and left. Our interest in pool had vanished and ashamed we bode the good inn keeper good-bye and returned to the school house. I can't even describe how depressed we were and I don't remember how we got back. The moment we returned we held an emergency meeting. It was decided to send the student in best standings with the principal as emissary to him and smooth things out. His mission seems to have failed. When we entered the dinning hall that evening, I thought I saw the principal smile at me. We did not like the dinner at all and I don't know how the others did that night, but I, for one, slept poorly.

Eight o'clock in the morning the written exams in theology began. Professor Alois's face was expressionless as he handed out the questions, but our faces grew longer and longer. We wrote and wrote. Noon came and none of us was finished. It was one o'clock before the first one turned in his exam, and some never finished up, because at two o'clock the next exam was waiting. That meant no lunch. The Greek language professor, who we teased earlier by taking his picture, gave us the Latin language exam on Tuesday. All went well and we thought that he had already forgotten everything.

On Wednesday the Greek language exam was on. When we stepped into the examination room the professor was ready: "Gentlemen, take out your Homer," he requested. We were somewhat astounded but followed his request. When everybody was ready he told us to open the book to a particular page and instructed us to translate fifty verses from Greek into Latin. The uproar was unbelievable, but when the professor kept smiling there was nothing else to do but obey.

This was quite a task and only four hours to do it. During the exam I turned halfway around and discovered that one of the students was using a cheat sheet, a booklet that contained German translations of the Greek text. With it, it wasn't difficult to translate the text into Latin. I didn't like what I saw; not just because it was dishonest, but also because my friend Karl who was weak in Greek, was certain to fail this exam. I decided to take the cheater for a ride, should my friend fail his exam. Everybody was sweating over the translation until two o'clock in the afternoon, and lunch was missed again.

The math professor was waiting for us, we thought, ready to torture us for another two hours of examination. But it turned out differently. The problems were easy and all of us were finished within an hour and a half.

After all the written exams were over, we met at the bowling alley to discuss the results. Later on our math teacher joined us. We were just discussing the Greek exams and the whole mess, when I saw my friend Karl with a rather sad look on his face.

I asked him how he did in the Greek exams: "Do you think you passed?"

"I don't know," he responded rather hopelessly.

This made me angry and I said loud enough for the math teacher to hear: "If you don't pass, Karl, I will make sure that the one who cheated won't pass either!" The teacher looked at me inquisitively and I repeated firmly: "And I mean it!"

The situation would be left at that until after the oral exams and the day we received our diplomas. The principal climbed on the high pulpit in the hall and made an elaborate speech. Afterwards one after another was called up to receive his diploma. I was as anxious to wait for Karl's diploma as for my own and when Karl's name was called I stood up as well. He did pass his exams and is today a well-respected priest.

Vacations at home were not what they used to be and I often stayed away. My dearest sister left home to earn money in some rich lady's service, my second sister worked as a maid, and my brother had to labor really hard. This was not my father's fault. I cannot and do not want to comment any further. I can only say that there were quite a few family spectacles when I did not come home for days, but instead stayed with relatives. My duty during vacations was to take care of my little half brother, my father's son from his second marriage. Being a student, I didn't like to be a nanny at all. Whoever still has a mother should thank God on his knees.

I had given up the idea of becoming a priest, because I much preferred my teachers' lifestyle, who belonged to the Sacred Heart Congregation. My father had no objections, but my step-mother did not quite agree with my decision. After my vacations were over, I entered the novitiate [period of being a novice]. Under the direction of a priest, Father Prevot, who died later in the call of piety, I conducted myself well. After the novitiate I was asked to teach in the very same school that I attended as a student for so many years. I taught Latin, two classes of history, and three classes of geography. In addition, I was appointed to monitor student activities off and on campus. My best friends were Professor Bocker, who took care of me and whose room I cleaned as a student, and Dr. Phillip, who is today the General

Superior of the cooperative of Sacred Heart priests with residence in Rome.

A year later, my interests turned toward philosophy and I was sent to Luxemburg where I began my courses at the Sacred Heart Monastery. I wasn't too fond of the situation there, though there was nothing wrong with the school or my studies. The studies were very hard, but in addition, I had to work as a nurse, which was no small chore. I spent all of my spare time in the ward; I even had to give up my weekly afternoon walks. The thought crossed my mind that I might be better off as a pastor, but I didn't share these thoughts with anybody.

After the second year of philosophy courses, we were permitted to spend our vacation in Clairefontaine, and an abbey near Luxemburg. We had a good time in this romantic valley and we could take hikes and walks to our hearts' content. Among other things, I remember well the Echternacher Spring procession:[1] five steps forward and three to the back in accordance to the music. After our vacation in Clairefontaine, we were allowed to go home for two weeks. I liked the idea that the people of my village would see me in my cassock and so I decided to go home.

My father had given up his carpentry and furniture shop. I don't want to elaborate on this but it hurt me to see my father, who was always independent, working as a wood sculptor for a big business. Today one can still visit the altar he made for one of the big churches in the Rhineland. It was just too hard for him to ride his bike in the mornings and evenings, to and from work. Taking my advice he quit that job, again started his own business and I decided to help out as best as I could. As a pastor, I thought, I would be able to help out.

I informed my Superiors of my decision not to return to school and since my agreement was to expire after the vacation, it was accepted. Now I had to see where I could find another job. To my great disappointment, by [German] government regulation, my secondary school diploma was not accepted because I attended school in Holland. Thus, it was a mistake to send me to that particular school. I could have repeated the exams under German regulations, but I wasn't ready for that. Consequently I hung up my cassock and tried to find a place to stay.

I found a place at a relative's home, the same relative I was waiting for all night at the train station years ago and for which I received quite a whipping from my father. Now she was married and we were still good friends. I was staying at her home when I was notified that I was accepted into the University of Fribourg, Switzerland. I had previously written to an old professor of mine, who eventually became a very good friend. He answered right away saying that if my report cards were all right I could come immediately [although he would already be late for the beginning of the semester]. All my report cards were good, indeed, excellent. So one evening, I took a train to Fribourg, where I arrived the following noon.

I took the few things I called my own and walked to the Salesianum—as the seminary was called[2]—where Dr. Joseph Beck, a Monsignor for quite some time, was the dean. A new segment in my life was to begin, and I was one step closer to the priesthood. I intended to work really hard so that I could finish my studies as soon as possible.

After my arrival I was taken into the office of the dean. His office was simple: a big table, some book shelves along the walls, two simple chairs, and a high pulpit behind which Dr. Beck was buried, absent-mindedly, in his studies. He was a big, broad shouldered man draped in a worn-out cassock, and I especially noticed his scrutinizing eyes, his vigorous mouth, and full, long black hair. After I introduced myself, he advised me abruptly of my room number and that I should report back this evening with all my papers in hand. That was an extremely short conversation and I wondered if I had left the right impression. When it is a matter of "to be or not to be," one's self-esteem is low, but I was back at the office at the requested time with my papers. Dr. Beck examined them closely.

"Very well," he said, "tomorrow you will begin your university classes."

Before I left he had one more question for me: "Why did you leave the Order of Sacred Heart?" He glared at me, waiting for an answer.

"I prefer to be a secular priest rather than a priest of the order," I responded, but I noticed that he was unsatisfied with my answer. I had not even started my courses at the university, and there was already some tension between my new Superior and me. I avoided him where ever and whenever I could.

Not surprisingly, life in the seminary was a communal affair. I immediately found a friend who was just as street-smart as I, and the two of us went through the seminary together until the end. Since he began his semester on time he was already adjusted to the environment, and I benefited immensely from that. Soon there were more and more friends, and I adjusted nicely. To be sure, university life was new to me. Depending on the schedule of our lectures we walked the twenty minutes from the Salesianum to the university. From the chancellor of the university I received my matriculation booklet to keep track of all my classes and grades. In this booklet, professors whose classes I took would confirm my attendance and attest to my successful passing of their classes or lectures. Those who skipped a few lectures were in danger of not receiving the professor's final approval.

The university in Fribourg is an international place. Students from all over the world enrolled here to take classes not only in theology but in other subjects as well. Many European and North American students were represented on this campus, but obviously most students came from Switzerland. All foreign nationals on this campus had a society to represent them. It did not take all too long until I was recruited by the German fraternity Markomania, or "Unitas Marcomania" as their banner announced it. The probationary period was one semester and almost every evening after dinner the young foxes, as we were called, gathered in the Fox Major's room and took lessons in college life. The Fox Major acted just like the priest in charge of Novices and the student's future quite often depended on him.

We were only allowed minimal contact with the senior fraternity boys, and only now and then were we allowed to participate in the weekly educational excursions. Initially we were only permitted to attend the fraternity's brunch meetings but as time went on we also participated in the afternoon events, applying what we had learned from the Fox Major. Official events happened only in the evenings and we foxes were not allowed to participate. Still, friendship and fraternity were well cultivated but academic studies were not neglected.

Some professors belonged to our fraternity and our faculty liaison was the famous and modest priest and excellent professor of Asian languages, Prince Max of Saxony, the brother of the then King of Saxony. I will never forget the good Prince Max. He owned his separate quarters near the Salesanium and we saw him quite often walking to the university. He always wore a too short and poor looking cassock. His valet, or servant, always walked about five steps behind him carrying his books and notes. Prince Max later gained fame when he tried to bring the Catholic and Oriental Churches closer together. He seemed to have gone too far, because Rome stepped in and Prince Max obediently acquiesced.

I listened to his lectures on liturgy and was tested by him in that field. It was the first and only time that I visited his office. It looked very simple and the only valuables in this office were his books. His table was so covered with books that there was no space for anything else. When he filled out my report card, he knelt down, used his chair as table, and then returned the paper to me.

The courses at the university weren't easy because all the lectures in theology were given in Latin. It didn't bother me much because my entire philosophy studies had been done in Latin. Only some of the professors, like the famous apologist Prof. Dr. Weiss, lectured in German and attracted the biggest crowd of students not only from theology and philosophy, but also from law and the arts.

University students usually showed their emotions in class. When a professor, who was well liked entered the lecture hall students would applaud. When a professor wasn't liked shuffling of feet on the floor could be heard. The same shuffling occurred when a professor went "overtime." Occasionally we skipped lectures, but only of those professors who had bad eyesight. When I attended university, exams were held in the respective professors' offices at the end of the semester.

I still remember Prof. Zapletal whose specialty was exegesis.[3] Most students avoided his classes in exegesis because his lectures and exams were very challenging. To pass his exams one had to know Greek and to translate and annotate a biblical text. When I arrived for my exam, he started by asking me if I knew Greek.

"I took four years of Greek," I told him.

When he gave me the Greek text and listened to my Greek translation, he soon interjected by asking me: "Where did you learn Greek?" I told him and we started a nice conversation which I tried to stretch as long as possible. After approximately half an hour he looked at his watch and said that the time was over. He filled out my report card with the grade "excellent."

Another time this strategy almost failed. As mentioned earlier, I stupidly thought that the dean of the Salesianum did not like me and therefore I tried to avoid him whenever possible. However, I could not avoid being examined by him. I think it was in Homiletic.[4] Since I was not familiar with his method, just about all my answers were wrong. The truth was, though, that I had never missed a lecture of his and he knew that I studied hard for his course. Therefore he sent me out with the words: "I will give you another eight days to prepare the material again and then re-examine you." That was very nice of him and even though I was ashamed, I came back after a week. I did pass and the dean patted me on the shoulder explaining "you see, coming back was for your own good." Since that time I liked Dr. Beck much more.

The last little bit of fear of him I lost at the end of that semester when we were ready to be fully initiated into the fraternity. The occasion was the final and festive commencement. It was an elaborate fest in which all professors and fraternities, with and without wearing their heraldic colors, participated. The whole affair lasted until midnight and many a student walked away very tired.

After the first semester break, some students noticed that the cafeteria food wasn't as good as during the previous semester. Criticism and dissatisfaction crept into the mood of the students. The issue came up among the fraternity members as well and it was discussed until I had had enough and said: "The food is no different from last semester. Those who complain are those who usually don't have enough at home." My words somehow reached the provost and he must have told the dean. Ever since the dean, Prof. Dr. Beck, and I were close friends.

I often accompanied Dean Prof. Dr. Beck, today Monsignor, from the Salesianum to the university. These walks made me understand the greatness of the Monsignor, and his love and concern for his students. I owe him all my gratitude for finishing the program, because whenever difficulties arose I went to him for advice and guidance over this rocky road. May God bless him a thousand times.

Quite often when a student thinks to have an advantage, he tries to profit from it. I have to admit, I, too, thought to use this situation to my benefit and it was certainly not nice of me. As mentioned earlier, I did not like it very much anymore at home, and I spent a lot of time with relatives instead. The closer the time came for my sub-deacon blessing, the deeper my thoughts developed and I came to a point where I just could not stand it anymore. I had to leave here for a while. The occasion came, when a great opera that I wanted to see, was to be performed. The decision was made and I wrote a letter to Anton and Gretchen, children of my aunt in Rheydt, with whom I stayed most of the time during my vacations. I did not mail the letter when doubts arose that Anton may not want to participate in my plan. I rewrote the letter and mailed it to Gretchen. The letter went something like this:

> You know that I will soon become a sub-deacon and then the nice times will be over. But before I take that step, I would like to have a little time to reflect carefully on this important step. I would like to come home, but I wouldn't be able to leave here. In addition, I would like to attend the opera which is showing a performance I haven't seen yet. If I were to come home, you and Anton might be able to go with me to Düsseldorf to see the opera. What do you think about that idea? If you like it, don't mind my little ruse and please do as I tell you. As you know your mother is sick quite often, and thus I was wondering if you could send me a telegram requesting me to come right away. This is the only way I can slip away from here. But then, should my little trick become exposed, I will be thrown out of the Salesianum, and that would be the end of that. So think about it, and don't talk to Anton about it, he goes too much by the book and doesn't do crooked things.

Three days later a telegram arrived requesting my presence: "Mother is sick, please come." Deep down in my heart I felt guilty, but I needed to get out. Consequently, I went to see the dean and sadly showed him the telegram. He agreed that I should leave right away. The next train from Fribourg via Basel along the Rhine to familiar surroundings was leaving in about an hour, at six o'clock in the evening. Some of my friends accompanied me to the station, where I invited them to a beer and then left. I was sad because of my lie.

When I arrived in the morning, my aunt was already waiting for me. I stayed with them for a few days and attended the opera, but I did not enjoy my stay as my guilty conscience was too strong. Eight or ten days later I returned to the university. After arriving in Fribourg, the Herr Dean, oblivious and very concerned, told me that he was very happy to have me back and that he advised the students daily to include my aunt in their prayers. I thanked him and reassured him that her ailment wasn't very serious and that those attacks occurred frequently. I truly deserved to be kicked out of the Salesianum. My aunt rests, for quite some years now, in the cemetery. She was for years a substitute for my dear mother and I will remember her always just as I will always remember my mother.

After every semester and before leaving for home, I took my exams. Not every student did his exams at the end of the semester, instead heading straight home. Throughout my university career my grades were good: optime (excellent), valde bene (very good), and only two grades with bene (good).

The house rules at the Salesianum were strictly observed and yet we enjoyed much freedom. It was custom, and tolerated by our faculty, that our fraternity had a day off during the week. As far as I remember our days off were Wednesdays. On that day at eight o'clock in the morning Prof. Dr. Beck held his lecture. We attended that one lecture regularly, returned home afterwards and exchanged our cassocks for civilian outfits. After adding our green-white-gold sash and yellow fraternity hats, we went down to the inn for a Frühschoppen [early brunch with wine or beer]. Lunch was required to be spent at the Salesianum and we had to change back into our clerical garb only to put on civilian cloths again afterward. Then we went generally for a long stroll to the outskirts of town, where a room for us students was reserved at an inn. All afternoon then we were in high spirits. In the evening we were back at the Salesianum for dinner. On particularly festive occasions we were allowed to stay out for the evening, but had to be back by midnight. We never thought of abusing that freedom.

Every afternoon after four o'clock, we were allowed to visit a friend in his room for a snack. We could have asked for an order-to-go from the cafeteria, but this would have had to be paid extra. Usually three of us got together, and alternately went into town to buy some ham or cheese, bread, coffee, and sugar. We had a little portable stove in our room on which we did some cooking. When we were finished, we washed dishes and returned to our respective rooms to study. After the communal prayers in the evenings, it was prohibited to enter another student's room and those who did not obey and were caught, were sent home on the first train the following morning.

Good companionship was helpful in preparing for exams. The most difficult exam for everybody who wanted to enter the priesthood was the cura animarum [management of theological life]. It was up to us to pick the examiner, either the dogma or ethics professor or the Herr Dean. I chose the latter. I was called into his office at eight o'clock in the evening. The topic of the examination covered the entire field of theology, thus the range of questions to be asked was endless. I was tested for two hours and I had to return at eight o'clock the following morning. I felt very good about the previous evening and my responses and entered Herr Dean's office with confidence.

Initially everything went fine. Questions and answers bounced back and forth. Suddenly the Herr Dean looked at me and asked with a twinkle in his eyes: "What is the second commandment of God?"

I looked at him with a baffled expression and tried to argue that this question was inappropriate for this exam.

"But why not?" and he repeated his question.

I was thinking and thinking but just couldn't find the answer.

"And you want to take confessions as a priest" he uttered, "but cannot even remember the second commandment?"

When he turned around to look at me he held his hand in front of his mouth. I was so stunned and confused, I felt like an idiot.

"Now it is all over and I've failed my exam," I thought, but the questions continued as if nothing had happened. After two hours the exam was over, and I had known everything but the Second Commandment. "I would have given you an optime—excellent—but I can give you only a valde bene—very good," commented Herr Dean while filling out my diploma. I was more than satisfied with my grade. After all, who can really expect an optime in a four-hour oral examination? The diploma had to be sent to the bishop.

With this piece of paper in hand, I ran back to the university to arrive just before class. My friends were waiting to hear the result. After presenting my diploma, I invited the entire fraternity to a Frühschoppen into our usual inn near the university. We celebrated until noon when it was time to return for lunch. I footed the bill, which was not cheap, but that didn't bother me in the least. All in all we skipped two lectures that morning. I was just happy to be done with this ordeal; it has happened that a student who didn't pass this last exam had to take all of them over again.

Time passed quickly and the priest ordination was coming closer and closer. I was to be ordained in the Cathedral in Cologne, my home diocese. The ordination was an unforgettable moment. When I left Fribourg, with blessings of the Herr Dean, the entire fraternity accompanied me to the train station. Since I had been a Fox Major in my fraternity for two semesters the corps assembled in full colors for my departure. I felt extremely honored. After a few rounds of beer, a brief goodbye and a promise to return for a visit to Fribourg, I boarded the train. I don't know how other students acted in situations like this, but everyone threw flower bouquets through the window into my compartment. I had tears in my eyes.

After eight days of preparation I was ordained in the Cathedral in Cologne and the next day I read already my first silent mass in a small church in Rheydt with only close relatives attending. This mass was in memory of my dear deceased mother and my father who scarified so much for me. On 19 March 1911, I joyously returned to my village. I had reached my goal.

During my years in the university, I not only majored in theology but also in economics. And I intended to advance my studies in economics. During my last university vacation I had attended already classes at the Volksverein für das katholische Deutschland[5] in Mönchengladbach. After a few days of rest [following his ordination] I started classes again. Out of convenience I stayed in Rheydt with relatives and commuted every morning at six o'clock by train to Mönchengladbach, which was twenty minutes away. There, before going to classes, I usually read mass. At the Volksverein, my instructors were the most famous German sociologists of the time: Dr. Braun, who later was elected to the Reichstag and Dr. Sonnenschein[6] considered the father of the labor movement, who brought more sunshine into the wretched workers' ghettos than the sun itself; and Dr. Nieder, the distinguished priest and famous scholar, who died at a very young age. The lectures lasted until noon, at which time I took the train home to study, only to return to school in the evening for discussions. Discussions usually lasted late into the night and I had to run to catch the last electric trolley to Rheydt.

The grand Cathedral of Cologne, one of the largest church buildings in the world, was the place of Father Küppers's ordination in 1911. Courtesy Palace of the Governors Photo Archives (NMHM/DCA), #155729

The work pace began to take its toll on my health. After a few weeks I had to rest and two lung doctors prescribed bed rest at a health resort and recommended I go to the best climate in the world for tuberculosis, namely New Mexico. I did not mention my trip to anyone but the closer the date of departure came the harder it was to leave.

One day I was called to Fribourg (as I will explain in the next chapter). This gave me the opportunity to keep my promise to return for a visit that I made to my fellow students before my departure from Fribourg. Prof. Dr. Beck gave the entire fraternity the day off and early in the morning we all boarded the train for the historic town of Mürten. There we had breakfast and some of us even took a bath in the nearby lake. In high spirits we embarked on a small ship which took us through the Mürten Channel and across Lake Neuchâtel to Neuchâtel. The only thing we had to concern ourselves with was our timely return to Mürten. We could not miss the last ship back because we had to be in the Salesianum by midnight. In the restaurant of the Palace of Neuchâtel we held court and turned the restaurant into a bar. The students had a great time, especially since I was the one paying the tab. Not surprisingly we forgot the time and all about the last ship back to Mürten. When I looked on my watch it was already five minutes too late. After I paid the bill we ran down to the lake as fast as we could but could already see our ship disappear in the far distance—a true sign that the earth is round.

It was difficult to know what to do next and all of us sobered up quickly. We knew very well that the Herr Dean would not take this transgression lightly since the students were supposed to be in bed by midnight. There was no train from Neuchâtel to Fribourg and swimming down the channel and across the lake to Mürten wasn't feasible either. Eventually I found a ferryman who, after some consideration and a fifteen francs pay-off, was willing to risk the trip and take us to the other side. The only condition he stipulated was that we sit still in the boat.

The whole situation was a tricky one. If, through carelessness, the boat was to keel over we all were going to drown. We were soon in the middle of the lake and our mood was improving, even though the boat was rocking quit strongly now and then. One of the students suddenly became seasick; probably not from the water since all he drank was beer. The boat rocked considerably and would have capsized, had it not been for the ferryman's quick-witted reaction to keep the boat in balance. When we turned from Lake Neuchâtel into the Mürten channel, one could hear a collective sigh of relief. At ten o'clock we arrived at Mürten where we ate a late dinner. Then we set out for Fribourg on foot, a four-hour walk, where we arrived dog-tired early in the morning. Now we had to sneak into the Salesianum without being noticed.

In front of the building I counted to see if all were present. Nobody was allowed to speak a word and just as we approached the front entrance, I had an idea: "Once we are safely in the building, you all go to sleep and I will stay up and wake you when the morning bell is sounding and calling us to the morning prayer in the chapel," I suggested, "but then you go back to bed and sleep as long as you want." I knocked quietly at the custodian's window that was promptly opened.

"You're all back?" he asked laughingly, "there will be a surprise waiting for you after breakfast."

"We had some bad luck," I responded while sliding a franc into his hand and all of us entered the Salesianum. One of the students ordered the removal of shoes and to go quietly onto their rooms. Everyone but me obeyed. I walked, guilt stricken, past the Herr Dean's room to go to my own room to think about the consequences. After fifteen minutes I checked every room of the late-night travelers to see if they were in bed. There was deep silence in some rooms, the sound of snoring in others, but no sign of guilt since I was the one who was responsible. Back in my room, I waited for the wake-up call. Then I ran from door to door to find out that a few were already up and others needed to be [woken up]. Those I grabbed by their collars and pull them, one at a time, out of bed. All students were present at the Morning Prayer, but most were missing at breakfast. After breakfast I went straight to the Herr Dean who received me with a somber expression. I told him what had happened and how we entered the Salesianum.

Then he said: "When you came in last night, I was standing in the window and overheard almost everything you said."

"Ha, ha, ha," he laughed with his strong voice. He asked if everybody came home safely and recommended, "the gentlemen should sleep in today." This was our good Herr Dean whom a smart student trusted unconditionally.

The following day I returned home with his blessing. I haven't seen him since in twenty-four years. In 1924 when I was in Europe to see my old father once more, I would have liked to go to Fribourg but was short of money. So I stayed at home until my vacation was over. I do have, though, a nice souvenir from the Herr Dean. When I boarded my ship in 1911, I was handed a big envelope. In it I found a photograph with the inscription Discilulo [sic] meo dilecto [sic] Reverendo Petro Küppers in memoriam—Prof. Dr. Joseph Beck.[7]

To New Mexico

Many foreign students, including quite a few Americans, attended the University of Fribourg in Switzerland. During my last years in Fribourg I got acquainted with them, many of whom spoke German, who told me a lot about America.

One day an American bishop visited Fribourg to recruit German theologians. The excitement was great and many graduates were accepted. I, too, was waiting to see the bishop, when I saw an applicant leaving his office rather confused.

"Don't go in there," he warned, "it isn't quite that easy to get comfortable with him," and added, "I cannot believe that this gentleman is a bishop. He's sitting in a big chair with both his feet on the table."

So I decided against signing up at that point but regretted my step shortly thereafter. I had heard so many nice things about the American bishop and I did want to go to America. The Dean of the Salesianum in Fribourg was helpful and promised to find another American bishop for me.

Two months later, a telegram arrived. I was called into the dean's office, where he informed me that I was accepted by an American bishop. After he translated the telegram for me into German, I almost fainted. It said: "The Archbishop of Santa Fe in New Mexico has accepted you into his diocese."

"But..., where is Santa Fe?" I stuttered. The Dean explained to me that Santa Fe was in the Southwestern part of the United States and that it will be a nice work environment for me. I wasn't sure if I was happy about this choice. I could not understand why of all places, I should go to New Mexico. I had a high opinion of myself and my grades were excellent. Today I understand that the Dean knew me well and that he chose the right place for me.

It wasn't easy to get used to the thought of living in New Mexico and the more I studied New Mexico's geography the less I liked the idea. But since I accepted the call already, I did not want to chicken out.

After my ordination, an event occurred that gave me hope and confidence. Archbishop Pitaval[1] was visiting Fribourg and I was asked by telegram to come to Fribourg. What a surprise it was to see a very affable gentleman in front of me. I could converse with him—poorly as it may have been—in French. When he handed me a $100 bill, the first one I had ever held in my hands, I asked him right away when he wanted me to leave for Santa Fe. "Take some time off," he told me, "and be in New York early in October," while writing down his address. In September I left from Antwerp [Netherlands].

The departure was not easy, but on the ship Lapland I quickly made friends. I never got seasick because I was very careful. [Once, however, he felt uncomfortable.] One Sunday morning I intended to hold mass on the ship but could not find my way to the captain's cabin. At ten o'clock when my stomach started to act up, I went on deck for a brief stroll but I felt the need to return to my cabin. Nothing happened as I went immediately to sleep only to wake up Monday morning. I had a good breakfast, and, unlike other passengers, never missed a meal during this stormy trip.

Once I almost fell into the ocean, or at least that's what a sailor on the ship thought. Towards the end of this trip, off the coast of Newfoundland, we sailed into a storm and experienced incredible rain. The ship rolled heavily up and down that one could barely remain on one's feet. We were ordered to stay below deck until the storm was over, but I didn't like the idea of being confined below deck. I wanted to know how the storm was coming along and decided to go on deck. Without further ado, I looked for a way out, and, indeed while holding on tightly, found my way to the highest deck. Barely there, a sailor grabbed me by the neck and with an appropriate seafaring curse, sent me right back below deck. There I stayed and felt just as comfortable as Jonas did in the whale's stomach. This event reminded me of the situation [told in an earlier chapter] that my father experienced swimming in the Rhine, shortly before he married my mother.

New York made a great impression on me. It wasn't so much the skyscrapers, though, than the first American breakfast. The ship dropped anchor late one Sunday evening. Those of us, who had no relatives awaiting them, could not leave the ship thus turning this into a long night. The next morning I boarded an American trolley pulled by horses and after a long ride was dropped off at the German immigration home.

I was very hungry but I could not finish the amount of food that was placed before me. I was served a big plate with a big hot something on it. I was told it was an American beefsteak along with potatoes, thick gravy, bread and butter, and apples and oranges. I immediately began to gobble down the meat, while others ate their fruit first. I have never seen a breakfast like that in Germany; Germans eat often and small portions.

"If America is always like that," I thought, "I'll be just fine here."
I was to learn soon, though, that New Mexico was different with its beans and Mexican [chile] pepper.

View of New York City in the 1910s as Father Küppers's may have seen it upon his arrival.
Courtesy Palace of the Governors Photo Archives (NMHM/DCA), #112701.

While in New York I didn't dare to leave the immigration home until a colleague took me under his wings and showed me, what I thought was the entire city. I always kept close to my guide, because I felt, once lost in New York, and you'll never find your way back. These masses of people! Whenever I bumped into someone I politely apologized in proper German: "I am sorry." I could not understand the English response but it sounded quite rude at times.

On one occasion, a conductor almost kicked me off the subway, or at least contemplated the move based to his facial expression. The fuss was all about my cigar, which I was smoking quietly and contently. The conductor's reaction seemed to me really picky and I never again used the subway system.

Eventually I met up with my archbishop in New York who told me to be in Santa Fe by the end of October. Again, he gave me money. Since I did not want to spend all my time in New York—I didn't feel safe there—I continued my travels.

I wanted to visit Philadelphia where I had friends and relatives. I don't remember how I got there. All I remember is that someone took me to the train and from then on, I was on my own. Nobody in the compartment wanted to talk to me. I was well versed in the German language but nobody seemed to be familiar with that language. When I heard the call "Philadelphia," and the train stopped, I got off the train. Immediately, a young boy with a red cap appropriated my travel bag without asking. I yelled a few choice words in German causing almost a ruckus before he returned my bag.

In front of the train station a few electric trolleys were waiting. I chose one and upon boarding said in German "To the Alfonsus Church." In turn, the conductor took me gently by the arm and put me back on the street. How inconsiderate! But I had to get there somehow! I tried the second trolley and this time I had more luck. The good conductor spoke German and after a long ride let me off at the designated place. There I reunited with the good pastor of the Alfonsus Church and his chaplain.

I was treated very well, only the beefsteaks were not quite as big as in New York and I feared that the farther I traveled inland, the smaller the portions might become. I had a nice time. All my colleagues, whom I got to know there quickly, were fine gentlemen and I spent many a nice day with them. I still cherish this time in my memories. Although I was still on vacation, I was expected to participate in the church's work. Eventually after two weeks, I ventured out by myself for the first time onto the streets visiting some colleagues. To my great surprise I also found a family who traced its ancestry back to my mother's family.

The day came when I had to leave for Santa Fe. I left on All Souls' Day from Philadelphia to Chicago. I didn't sleep all night because there was so much noise on the train. When the train made a stop, I believe in Pittsburgh, I nearly suffocated from the smog and pollution of nearby factories. As far as I can remember, I arrived in Chicago in the evening and wanted to continue to Cudahy, Wisconsin, where a fellow student of mine was living.

Nobody at the ticket counter in Chicago wanted to sell me a ticket and I was referred from one counter to the next. How I made my connection, I don't remember, but I was pretty furious that nobody in the United States spoke and understood a little bit of German.

At one of the stops I heard someone shout "Milwaukee." Only one man left the train and I followed. It was a small station, and I knew I was in the wrong place. Based on previous experiences, I did not feel like asking for help. I followed the man at a respectful distance until he suddenly stopped and waited. I did the same. A trolley approached, I boarded it and luckily it let me off right in front of the entrance of a church. I glanced toward the gate and saw my old friend from Fribourg standing there. In my excitement of seeing him I almost hurt myself. When I jumped off the tram in a hurry, I fell over my travel bag and landed two meters farther in the mud.

I stayed for three days to dry out and when it was time to go on, my friend took me to the station and bought me the ticket to Santa Fe. At the ticket counter he asked me if I wanted to travel in a Pullman. Too ashamed to admit my ignorance about what a Pullman was (although I had used one between Philadelphia and Chicago) I responded brusquely: "No, no I don't want that." Had he asked if I wanted a sleeping car, I would have understood, but for a Pullman, I was too stupid. Such is life if one doesn't know the language.

I took my seat in the so-called "chair car" and was on my way to Santa Fe. The ride wasn't very comfortable and I didn't get much sleep at all. The next day, once we were past Kansas City, the scenery turned somewhat desolate and aside from that, my heart and stomach turned queasy for I missed breakfast in Kansas City.

During that last stop in Kansas City, I saw many people leaving the train [to have breakfast], but some stayed, and again I tried to pretend to be a know-it-all and remained, too. I couldn't understand why so many people left the train only to return half an hour later. When I visited Kansas City again years later, I thought I was lucky at the time not to have left the train, or else I would have gotten lost in this huge train station.

When the train arrived in Newton, Kansas, the conductor shouted again something I did not understand, but I noticed that the same motion set in. I looked out the window and saw where the people went. I quickly followed them, just in time to get a table in the restaurant. The waitresses in the restaurant were well dressed and polite—even to me. As usual I couldn't understand a word the waitresses were saying, and motioned instead to bring me the same food as my neighbor had ordered. The result was a good slice of meatloaf, potatoes, and peas. After I finished off my plate, coffee and a piece of cake were served. Now I understood the system and never again missed a meal.

The second night on the train was worse than the first one and the closer I came to Santa Fe the more lightheaded I became. Near Trinidad, Colorado, I had another scare. On some small train station a man boarded the train, greeted me friendly, and sat down next to me on an empty seat. He spoke to me in a language other than English. It must have been Spanish and Spanish was like Greek to me, so we looked at each other rather moronically. On this long journey nobody had talked to me to this point and thus, I was very thankful from the bottom of my heart for his attempts to make conversation with me, and I thought, if all Mexicans are like him, it will be just fine working for them. This thought put me at ease for a while, but my good mood did not last very long.

From Colorado, the train entered through the Raton Pass into New Mexico, which appeared to me rather desperate and desolate. When I saw the first adobe huts, I couldn't believe that people actually lived in them. These were small buildings with generally only one door, a few little windows and a deplorable roof. The skyscrapers in New York and Chicago impressed me, though I would not want to live in them. "Lion and mouse" came to mind when comparing the skyscrapers to these adobe huts.

Whenever the train stopped, I looked curiously out the window only to be disappointed with what I saw. My mood received a lift when I arrived in Las Vegas. This little town looked pretty reasonable, at least the parts that I could see from the train station. I noticed quite a number of Mexicans who did not seem to have anything to do. I did like those guys, though. When the train came to a standstill, I stepped off the car and strolled like the other passengers up and down the platform. Nobody greeted me, but the Mexicans nodded friendly as if they had known me for years.

When the train reached the vicinity of Lamy, the conductor came by to have a conversation with me, which turned into a minor calamity. Once he tried it in English and then in Spanish, which was worse. I shook my head but he kept trying and when the train came to a halt, he grabbed my hat and travel bag and took me by my arm. I was forced to follow him. I was afraid he might kick me off the train.

The train station at Lamy station, ca. 1912, was Father Küppers final stop before arriving in Santa Fe. Courtesy Palace of the Governors Photo Archives (NMHM/DCA), #61669.

Once outside, he pointed to another train and I understood: I had to switch trains. When I walked along the railroad tracks to catch the other train I became discouraged again because I saw something I had never seen before. By now I had seen adobe houses, but nothing like those in Lamy: A few posts were driven into the ground and covered with mud, and a few tiny windows blended in. The roof consisted of thin beams, also covered with mud. Some dogs were chasing me and for the first time I made use of the umbrella I brought from Germany. I hurried to reach the train. I had never seen a train like it: a small engine, only two wagons for passengers, and a tiny freight car for merchandise and goods.

I was terrified on the one-hour trip to Santa Fe. The little train rattled and shook so much, that I expected it to derail any moment. Other passengers, however, appeared so detached that I pretended serenity as well but thought of repentance and misery. Finally the conductor shouted "Santa Fe" and my journey was finally over.

Somebody yelled at me as I left the train, but I didn't pay him any attention. When he saw my Roman collar, however, he lifted his hat and greeted friendly.

Another man came, equally friendly, and took my luggage. I was so confused and tired and had no clue what was said that I didn't care anymore, but whispered "Pitaval," the name of the Archbishop of Santa Fe. Without any hesitation he pushed me into a waiting carriage, closed the door, and off we went.

The horses went as fast as they could and when the carriage came to a halt, the door was opened and I jumped out. The teamster said something but I only understood the name Pitaval. I didn't see a house, only a long adobe wall with a flimsy gate. The teamster tried to open it and the thought crossed my mind that an archbishop wouldn't live here. He even tried climbing the gate. By that time I was wondering about that man and kept my umbrella, my only weapon, handy, just in case. After he gave up opening the gate, he returned respectfully lifting his hat and laughed. He pushed me back into the carriage and, after a few hundred yards, pulled over again and took my suitcase.

When we reached the entrance, the driver pushed me through the door where, to my big surprise, an old but agile priest welcomed me in French: "We expected you a long time ago." I was so astonished that I couldn't say a word. Another priest entered the room who repeated the welcome in German. I think had I not been a newcomer here, I would have received a penance already, perhaps with three days of spiritual exercises. Instead, the priest took me to a nearby small house, furnished with a kitchen and a dining room. The table was still set but because the food was cold, it did not taste very good. The priest poured me a glass of wine from an open bottle, but to make a good impression I declined politely although the wine would have been the best part of the entire meal.

After dinner he showed me to a little room, bade me good night, and disappeared. So, I thought, this is home! I sat down on the only chair, took out a photograph of my mother and father, and made up my mind to leave this place behind as soon as possible. Had I had the necessary cash, I would have left that same night toward homier areas, but all I could do was to go to bed.

Life in Santa Fe, New Mexico

Germans from childhood on are used to eating sauerkraut with a stein of beer or a glass of buttermilk, Irish eat their potatoes unpeeled, and the French finish a meal of dumplings with wine. As long as my intentions were to become a Mexican priest, I had to become accustomed to new and unfamiliar conventions which I didn't like one bit.

I couldn't sleep at all that first night. First, my bed in the shadow of the cathedral of Santa Fe was very primitive; second, I was so homesick I shivered; and third, I missed the fat beefsteaks of the early days in the immigrant home in New York. The last point was confirmed at breakfast the next morning.

Breakfast consisted of one fried egg, bread, and a cup of coffee which smelled suspiciously like chicory.[1] Lunch wasn't so bad; at least the priest and his two chaplains seemed to think so. Indeed, the soup was excellent and, like the other gentlemen, I filled up my plate with beans, because I was very hungry. I topped off the beans with a red sauce containing little cubes of beef. Unsuspecting any maliciousness, I tasted the food and thought it was a bad joke. The red stuff was seasoned with so much pepper I choked and shed quite some tears. Since I was still new here and wanted to please the gentlemen, I bravely swallowed this stuff. Whenever I felt unobserved I used my napkin to dry tears from my eyes.

I did not participate in the conversation, which was in French, as I didn't want to embarrass myself and besides I was busy conquering the pepper which the gentlemen called 'chile.' Finally the priest asked: "Did you like lunch?" Not wanting to lie and not being able to express my feelings well enough in French, I pulled out my last ace and responded in Latin: "De gustibus no est disputandum," meaning one cannot argue about taste. Everybody started laughing and the old gentleman, patting me on the shoulder, said: "You will make a fine priest in New Mexico." Ever since, I was the old man's favorite priest.

This was to my advantage because he was second in rank after the Archbishop of Santa Fe. I have to admit that the old guy, Monsignor Fourchegu[2], was a strong, robust man; now and then he was a little unsophisticated but his heart was in the right place, just like God would want a man. He was promoted to Monsignor because of his tremendous missionary work in New Mexico. He did not write books and never hid behind a desk, yet he rose to become a clerical dignitary.

Monsignor Antoine Fourchegu, ca. 1911, was popular in Santa Fe and Father Küppers was fond of the burly cleric. Courtesy Palace of the Governors Photo Archives (NMHM/DCA), #43085.

I never did like the meals at the cathedral—just as my priest from the Guadalupe Church had predicted. The housekeeper in the presbytery was Spanish.

Later, as one of his chaplains, I received an early morning call to a sick man's bedside. On the way out of the rectory, I had to pass the Monsignor's room and saw the light on. Somewhat concerned, I knocked at his door and heard his deep voice bellowing along the hallway "Come in." I could not believe my eyes and stumbled an apology: "I thought you might be sick."

"Sick?" he wondered surprised, "I am just saying my breviary which I do every morning at four o'clock. Then I smoke a cigar (he always smoked Stogies, a penny apiece), reflect, and then I am ready for mass. That way I have all day to attend to my congregation." I didn't say a word and left deeply embarrassed for my sick call. I intended to follow his example but after three days I slept in again rather than get up at four o'clock.

When the archbishop finally arrived in Santa Fe, he must have received a good report about me because when I visited with him he was just as friendly as at our first meeting in Fribourg. He encouraged me to learn English and Spanish. I explained to him that I developed a system of learning the languages:

> "Whenever I go for a walk taking pictures with my camera, or when I go shopping, I make conversation, and I look for the appropriate words in the dictionary. That way I make new friends and learn English."

I didn't say much about my progress with the Spanish language because I just could not figure out how to learn two languages at the same time. Still, I felt more and more at home.

Once, though, when I felt melancholic I almost got in trouble. This happened during my first Christmas in New Mexico. Back home we always had a huge Christmas tree where young and old gathered around, sang the most beautiful Christmas carols, and exchanged gifts. This Christmas Eve I had to walk to St. Catherine's Indian School, about two miles from the cathedral. It was already dark when I took my walking cane and filled my pockets with stones to protect myself against barking dogs. I don't know how many stones I threw at them once I passed the last houses in the street, but my arm was lame and hurt. By the time I arrived at the Sisters and conducted the festivities at the monastery's church, my mood was at rock bottom.

The following morning, I attended the Pontifical Mass and had lunch at the Cathedral. The food felt cold despite the fact that it came right off the stove. I decided I needed to celebrate a warmhearted Christmas. I knew a German family whose father was a shoemaker for the Indian School [on Cerrillos Road]. I grabbed my hat and walking stick and left the house. For the shoemaker I took along cigars, which I had bought for myself before Christmas. I also brought along a few pounds of sugar. To remain unnoticed, I left through a side entrance. When I arrived at the family's home I learned that, except for something from the Indian School, the [shoemaker's] children received no Christmas gift. It was really sad and yet, this was perhaps my most enjoyable Christmas I have ever celebrated and I think it was because this was the first one I attended out of compassion.

Archbishop Lamy blessed and dedicated the building 1887 and St. Catherine's Indian School accepted its first students the same year. Courtesy Palace of the Governors Photo Archives (NMHM/DCA), #3269.

About five o'clock I returned home to my room. At the cathedral I ran into the First Chaplain who without hesitation hollered in German: "Where have you been? You were supposed to put away the vestments today! I had to do everything myself." I was so surprised that I didn't know what to say and gave him a chance to continue. "This idleness has to stop now," he barked at me, "and when you leave the house the next time I want you to inform the Father or me." I thought, why aggravate the gentleman even more so instead said politely: "Merry Christmas, dear Colleague."

In his bewilderment he held on to the doorpost to prevent falling over. I left him standing there and went to my room. I locked my door so nobody could bother me and had a frank conversation with the Lord. By the time the bell rang for dinner, I felt indisposed. Long after I forgave the chaplain for his little verbal attack but his remarks about idleness stuck with me.

I was doubly alarmed by this characterization when one day a new priest arrived on horseback and introduced himself and his horse. He told me that he was chaplain in a rural parish but was called to Santa Fe by the Archbishop. "Something is happening and I don't know what," I thought. I was afraid that the new priest might become chaplain at the cathedral. He knew German, French, English, and Spanish. I aspired to become a chaplain at the cathedral, and without hesitation I went to see the archbishop and stated my demands clearly: "I want to be chaplain at the cathedral!"

I think His Excellency has never been as surprised as at that moment. But he did not let on, and instead, calmed me down and explained: "I have chosen you for a nice and challenging place and will soon send you there. Until then, study eagerly English and Spanish." I returned to my room and locked myself in again. I wasn't angry like on Christmas day. Rather, I felt ashamed and when it was time for dinner I really felt bad.

The next morning at breakfast, the archbishop came by and sat down to talk with me. When he was finished, I knew that I was promoted to chaplain and transferred to the Guadalupe Church. I was asked to start there the same day—this meant the end to my leisure time.

The Guadalupe Church is the second church in Santa Fe. The transfer from the cathedral where I had a prestigious position for two months, to another church was a demotion. The priest's reception at the Guadalupe Church was initially cool.

He told me immediately: "I am always the one who gets stuck with the German assistants."

My face turning red and shot back: "It wasn't my choice to come here either; I wanted to stay at the cathedral."

"And if you don't want me," I continued, "I'll turn around and go home. I have enough of New Mexico anyway."

"Just stay here," he laughed, "the Germans are good workers." I was forever thankful and although I did my novitiate with him, it was the merriest year I have ever spent in New Mexico.

I still spoke only very little Spanish but without any notice and barely a week into my new position, the priest took me to the church and introduced me to the assembled children. He ordered me to teach them the catechism in Spanish and then left me alone with of all these kids. This obviously was all Greek to me[3], but I took the catechism and slowly read the prayers aloud over and over again. By the end of the hour I knew already "The Lord's Prayer" and "Ave Maria" in Spanish.

Every Thursday I joined the priest on his horse and buggy rides to the state penitentiary. The horse, however, was afraid of automobiles. I, too, was scared to death of the few automobiles that were already driving around in Santa Fe at the time.

Monday evenings we taught a religion course in English at the government's Indian School. The school was just outside of Santa Fe and after we went there a few times together, the priest told me: "The next time you'll hold the class by yourself." I objected on the account that I didn't know enough English yet.

"Then you have to learn it," he said and gave me a catechism with English annotations. I studied every evening until late into the night.

The day to teach came. Since I didn't know how to handle the horse and carriage a little Mexican boy came along. Four hundred Indian children assembled in the auditorium for their spiritual education. To keep order in the hall, there were always several teachers present. My heart beating fast, I stepped up to the podium, made the sign of the cross and in the German language—stuttered a prayer. Nobody understood a word I said, because I lost my composure. The remainder of the lesson went well because I memorized most of my lecture. When I was stuck, I looked into the book.

After three weeks on the job I was already expected to preach both in English and Spanish. Every Monday morning I wrote a sermon from a prayer book, one in English and another one in Spanish. Across from the rectory lived a German family and a French woman who was married to a Spaniard. Then I took the English sermon over to the German family whose daughter who was a teacher and spoke English well. I read the sermon aloud to her. Then I memorized her corrected version and presented it every Friday and Saturday. Still, despite all my good intentions, people in the congregation often laughed.

I did the same with my Spanish sermon. I went over to the French-Spanish family, and the woman who spoke excellent Spanish helped me faithfully. Since I knew German and some French I quickly became familiar with the mistakes she detected. This way I learned the languages very fast and after a few months wasn't intimidated anymore.

The parish priest was in charge of the sick and often traveled to far away places. The farthest place was about eighty miles away.[4] One Saturday evening a sick call came. The railroad stopped three miles short of a woman's place and because it was Saturday, I had to go. I was given all the necessary directions. The priest accompanied me to the station, purchased a ticket for me and saw me off. I reached the final stop at around ten o'clock in the evening where I was supposed to be met by a man in a buggy. When I got off the train, not a soul was there and everything was pitch dark. I walked slowly down the village street with my little handbag in my left hand and the right hand at my chest where I held hidden the dear Lord's cross. I saw a small chapel where a man addressed me in Spanish. I tried my best to understand him, but he rattled down some Spanish phrases so fast, I had not a clue what he said. To get away from him I answered in Spanish "yes, yes, si, si." Instead, he took my arm, lead me to his buggy, and off we went. It was so dark, we had to go slow and I noticed, we were driving very close to a ravine, but I wasn't scared.

Finally we arrived at a house where I was motioned to step off the buggy. How surprised was I when I entered the house. There was only one room with a door leading to what appeared to be the kitchen. A solid wooden bed stood in a corner and next to it an empty wobbly old chair. In the opposite corner on the floor, a person was laying on an old mattress surrounded by kneeling women. Some of the women must have been smoking as I entered the room because several still lit cigarette butts covered the floor. I said my greetings in Spanish and quickly approached the sick woman. The women showed no intentions of getting up to leave the room but making a sign to leave me alone with the sick woman worked. I don't know how I communicated with her, but we understood each other—at least in the bare essentials. After confession, there was nothing else for me to do, as she wasn't sick enough to receive her Holy Communion. I pulled out my Spanish prayer book, let the waiting people return, and prayed with them until a few minutes past midnight. By then the sick woman was at least sober enough to receive the Holy Communion.

Unfortunately, it was explained to me, I had now missed the last train. In desperation I sat down on the fragile old chair next to the bed and contemplated my situation. Then it came to me that if I had to stay here, I had to sleep somewhere. Since nobody seemed to offer to help me, I pointed to the bed, which brought the group into motion. Some left the room and others, I think the woman's relatives, began pulling about six mattresses off the bed. They spread one after another out on the floor but left one on the bed which they covered with white linen, a blanket and a round pillow. They indicated that this would be my bed and left the room. I went to bed immediately but as a precaution I left my pants and socks on. I was barely in bed when the assembly came back and one after another laid down on the remaining mattresses. The entire situation was so new to me that I kept one eye open. I could not go to sleep immediately and pondered about the life of these poor people and how those with earthly goods should be thankful to receive such favors from God. Many of them, in my opinion, do not deserve it.

The next morning I couldn't hold mass [in Santa Fe] because I had missed the train the night before. When I woke up, everybody but the sick woman who was still sleeping, was gone. I tried in vain to figure out a way to notify the people here to come to the chapel for a few prayers. Instead, I took my time getting up, said a short prayer, and went in search for a cup of coffee. Coffee was already brewing in the small kitchen and a big tortilla (hard bread baked on the stove) was waiting for me. The same man who brought me here took me back to the train and I arrived safely in Santa Fe. I will never forget this first experience. Now I felt like a true priest and was happy to work among the poor.

The following week relatives in France notified the priest at the Guadalupe church that his father was ailing and that it was necessary for him to go to France. He left the following Sunday and left me in charge of the parish. I wasn't keen about this assignment, but I had no choice.

The reason why I did not like the job was that the priest was in the process of building a new rectory and we had to make do with makeshift quarters. The priest had moved into the sacristy while I resided in a converted stable equipped with a kitchen and a small dining room. The old housekeeper came by every morning and left in the evening. To continue this construction of the rectory seemed impossible to me. When the priest reassured me that he did not expect me to work on the rectory, I calmed down.

With the priest's departure my labor and grief began. I would have preferred death had that whole time not been so comical. Now that I was in charge, I wanted to save as much money as I could and my first decision was to let the little Mexican boy who always helped with the horses, go. I thought I could handle the horse by myself.

Like every Thursday evening I harnessed the horse to drive to the state penitentiary. I felt brave but suddenly, a short distance ahead of me several red lights appeared. I didn't know the meaning of that but when the horse approached the lights, it suddenly stopped. I used the whip and that moment, the horse jerked and I flew out of the buggy, landing in a nearby ravine. Unhurt but screaming I worked my way out of the ditch. I heard some noise on the adjacent property as if something crashed.

Still screaming I ran into the dark farmyard where I almost ran into a family—father, mother, and daughter. They recognized me immediately and the father went to get a lantern. We inspected the disaster. The red lights meant that the road was closed and a big ditch interrupted the road. When I whipped the horse it jumped across the ditch, then the buggy and I followed with a somersault. The horse escaped into the family's farmyard, in the process running over a small outbuilding situated near the main house, and waited there in a corner for things to come. Since nobody was hurt, the good man helped harness the horse but I did not dare to get into the buggy and instead walked the horse to the penitentiary to fulfill my duties among the prisoners.

But how would I get back home? I knew an alternate route along the railroad tracks. To be the safe, I walked the horse again. Halfway home the bright light of a train came toward us. In panic I stepped bravely in front of the horse and held on to the reins with both hands. The horse tried to stand on its hind legs but I held on until the small Santa Fe-Lamy train passed. Horse, buggy, and I were saved! I was nervous for a few days, but I gave the little boy his job back immediately.

The following Monday I was about to go to the Indian School when the Presbyterian minister drove up in his buggy and offered me a ride to the school. He taught some Presbyterian Indian children there but I did not make any fuss about it. Over the course of the year he often picked me up and took me along to the school. We have always been good friends and I valued him highly. He left the church eventually, I think, to accept a more lucrative job. He told me so himself—he hadn't forgotten me—when I ran into him once in Tucson, Arizona.

Thursday came around and it was time again to pay my visit to the penitentiary. But I did not want to admit that I was scared to go by myself in the buggy. Now I had this genius idea to place two wide and heavy boards on the axles underneath the buggy sticking out in the back about a foot and a half. This was enough space for me to stand instead of sitting in the buggy. With heavy wire I tied the boards down to the axles so that they wouldn't move. All this I did in secrecy. When the boy harnessed the horse that evening I was in good spirits and instead of climbing into the buggy I took the reins and stepped onto the boards behind the buggy. The boy looked at me as if I had lost my mind. Yet, the ride to the penitentiary went well and in the dark nobody paid much attention to my unique contraption.

After one hour I returned home the same way. I was just about to turn into the gate at home when the horse stumbled, got spooked, and sped up. This caught me by surprise and I fell backwards off the boards. The horse ran to the stable where I finally caught up. Since the boy had not yet come out of the house, I began to unhitch the horse as if nothing happened. That night I did not sleep at all but [out of frustration] wished the entire priest system would go to "some other place."

Next morning I sought comfort from the priest of the cathedral. I told him everything and he reassured me that I will learn [how to handle a carriage] and that everything will turn out just fine. I voiced my desire to buy a riding horse rather than to labor with the buggy and the stupid white horse. He laughed heartily and after a moment of silence he responded:

"I will sell you my horse; it is well behaved and docile, and I can always buy another one if need be. Then you'll have a rather tame animal."

I knew his horse was truly docile. I have seen the priest on this horse many times in the streets of Santa Fe and it behaved as if hitched to a milk cart trying to stop at every house. The old mare's discipline, however, derived from years of making house calls with the priest. I bought the horse for the reasonable price of $15, which I was to pay that same afternoon. The priest took me to the stable where I took the horse by the rein ready to lead it home.

The priest, however, insisted: "Get up on the horse and ride home; here's a saddle as well."

"No thank you," I responded apologetically, "I will try it out at home."

I wished I had listened to him, because in that case, I would not have bought the horse at all. On my way home, it was truly a pain to keep the horse moving—to the full enjoyment of my audience—because of its stupid habit to stop at every house as if harnessed into a milk cart.

On the way back to Guadalupe I passed a German with whom I was acquainted for some time and who fought bravely as a Rough Rider under Roosevelt in San Juan.

This guy yelled in German: "Father, does your horse suffer from consumption?"

That was scorn, and I bellowed back: "Had you been on a horse like that in San Juan, you'd be dead."

Had I known English better, I would have embarrassed him in front of all the people.

Back at the rectory I took the horse into the stable and put the saddle on. I called the boy and told him to hold the horse: "Stay in front of the horse and don't let go until I say so." I mounted the horse, but instead of going forward that stupid animal went backwards and started bucking. It kicked the buggy, which happened to be parked in the doorway, broke its shaft and tried to retreat further and further. I scream at the boy: "Don't let go, hold on and pull! Pull!" but it was already too late. I was caught between the horse's neck and the door beam. I don't remember what I screamed in that moment of panic, but the boy let the rein go. The horse moved forward and I fell off the horse to the ground. The saddled horse went straight back to its previous master using San Francisco Avenue. I followed on a different route and returned to the cathedral. I returned the horse, which was easy since I hadn't yet paid the $15.00. I had my saddle returned a few days later. As with everything, getting used to new things took time; but within a few weeks I learned how to handle horses and drove the buggy all by myself to even far away missions.

Once, after the Guadalupe Church priest's return from France, something rather odd happened. I had to visit the missions and planned on staying out for a few days. After I finished my visit to the nearest missions, I went to the mission in Golden about 40 miles south of Santa Fe. I arrived on time and at four in the afternoon entered the small public school building to teach religion. The next morning I read mass in the small chapel, had breakfast, and left the village for Santa Fe the same way I came. Just outside the village stood a man in civilian clothes, but I noticed a star on his chest. "Something is cooking," I thought and it turned out to be true. The man represented the local police and likely had some ax to grind with the Catholic Church because just when I was about to pass speedily by him, he grabbed the reins and forced me to stop.

"Let go of my horse," I yelled at him. I had a shotgun in the buggy but it was out of reach.

"You can't leave the village, you will have to stay a few days; this place is under quarantine," he replied. "We have an outbreak of measles."

"Do you have the measles, too?" I asked him. The local peace officer turned almost irate but I knocked him down a notch or two.

"If you can't show any respect for the law, I'll arrest you."

"Do you know who I am?"

"I don't care who you are," he contended, "but you will obey the law."

The word "law" has many meanings in New Mexico, especially when a scoundrel was the guardian of the law. I wasn't afraid, but there was no need to upset that guy any more.

I asked him: "Do you have all your marbles, where is the logic here?" He surely would have turned wild had he understood either the meaning of marbles here or what logic meant. Instead, I explain:

"Why did you let me into the village? You should have told me yesterday afternoon that you and the others have measles. Besides, why is the school not closed? And also, I should not have read mass to avoid congregating people. If you don't let me pass I'll report you to the authorities."

"I am the authority and you will turn around," was his answer. This guy was capable of shooting me had I decided to run his road block. So, I turned around. When I arrived again at my host's house, he looked surprised. "Lazarus," I asked him, "do you have any common sense? Why didn't you tell me that there is a measles epidemic in town?"

"No," he said, "I don't have measles."

I could not be angry with him; he was a very good old man. Instead, I told him: "Get into the buggy and come along; I'll explain everything on the way."

Lazarus was grinning because he knew what was going on. But he, too, did not say a word to me. When he saw me trying to leave town into the opposite direction, he told me, "there's a policeman too; we won't get through." For the moment I did not know what to do. "Stay in the buggy and when the danger is passed, you can walk home." We turned around, passed the little church, and drove through a dried-out riverbed up the hill. When we left the village behind us unnoticed, I said to Lazarus:

> "Please, for once, be nice, Lazarus, come with me to the next train station some twenty miles from here. If we hurry I'll catch the train to Santa Fe and be home by five or six. Then you'll take back my buggy but make sure you arrive in the dark or else you might get caught. Tomorrow morning bring the horse and buggy back to Santa Fe. If everything turns out ok, I will treat you well in Santa Fe."

We then rode on a pretty decent road to the station, and as so often I was in luck. I took the train and Lazarus brought the buggy and the horse safely back to Santa Fe the next day.

The priest praised me for my quick senses but I was generally good in getting out of a jam. Lazarus got a railroad ticket back, but the poor man had to walk the last twenty miles from the end station to Golden. (This story actually doesn't belong here but since I was talking about horses, I thought I should place it here.)

I was very happy as the assistant priest but I was even happier when I could show my fighting spirits. As it often happens, when the priest leaves the parish for a few days, those who don't like the priest take this opportunity to make it difficult for him. This parish was no different. I was a young priest, barely out of the seminary, and not very experienced in handling difficulties. Rumor was spreading that the priest left, not because he was called home, but because he supposedly embezzled money from the parish. This was strange and since it was only a rumor I did not pay too much attention. But I was prepared to give my full support to the priest and if necessary, expose the slanderer.

One morning I went to see the archbishop in hope of getting some specific information. In my discussion with him, I mentioned casually the parish and the priest. But I did not find out anything and I did not want to ask straight out to avoid putting my foot in my mouth. I was about to leave again when the archbishop asked me to announce that he will visit the Guadalupe parish next week and after High Mass will speak to the congregation. "Aha," I thought, "something is not right."

Had I just thought of checking the books, nothing at all would have come of it, because the priest was innocent, as it turned out shortly. Sunday came, and it was raining cats and dogs. Before High Mass I was sitting in my office lost in thought, when someone knocked at the door and the archbishop entered. I was confused and he noticed it too, when I said: "Today not many people will come to mass, it is raining so miserably." In turn, he asked: "Did you announce my upcoming visit last week?" "Oh God," I moaned, "I forgot all about that," and I really did.

This was not a good start for reading mass. I began awkwardly reading the mass or as it is called in Latin Coram Espiscopo. After I recited the Evangelium in a rather meek voice, the archbishop stepped up and I had to sit down. The first thing he said was that I earned a reprimand for not announcing his visit at last week's service. I felt sick to my stomach and wished to be chaplain rather than the acting priest. Then he came right to the point that he heard complaints that money was misappropriated— money which was collected for the construction of the new church. He emphasized that he did not believe that there was any truth to that rumor, but would check the books upon the pastor's return. This statement was a relief for me. In order to prevent further rumors in the future, the archbishop announced the formation of a commission or a board that will administer the monies and remain in place after the pastor's return. Now I felt like an idiot! I was so confused I don't know how I finished mass. Very confused, I answered briefly the few questions the archbishop asked me after the service. There was no discussion about my forgetfulness.

Instead, he told me: "When I give an order I expect prompt execution, please."

He continued: "I will immediately appoint the board and have its president speak to the people next Sunday."

I did not say anything, but was about to cry.

I hadn't heard a thing all week. And on Sunday before the service, the newly appointed president had me announce that he will speak to the congregation after completion of the service. I did not respond because I was prepared. All week long I went through the books and checked every number and every amount. If he will find any pretense of wrong doing against my priest, I'll make trouble. During High

Mass I did not read the Evangelium nor did I preach but went straight to the sacristy. I left the door slightly ajar and positioned myself in a way that I could not be seen but could hear everything.

The president spoke so fast and my Spanish was so poor that I understood very little. But when he was finished I knew who the remaining board members were. They were good men of the best families and all were friends of mine. Among them was a Pennsylvania Dutch who was a member of my congregation and with whom I could converse easily in German. When everything was over, I immediately requested a first board meeting for seven o'clock that night in my office and indicated that even the Archbishop might show up.

Why wait for the return of the priest. Instead, I took the heavy ledgers and went to see the archbishop. Everything is documented in the books. "Good," said the archbishop, "did you check the books?" I showed him that the books were clean. There was a small discrepancy of eleven dollars, which would hardly be enough to take off to France. He laughed and replied: "I am pleased that you are firmly defending your priest."

I did not mention a word about the upcoming board meeting that night. I went home and at seven o'clock sharp all board members, all of them my friends; only the president was missing. I told my friend, the Pennsylvania Dutch man, that I will speak in German and that he would need to translate. Then I told them that I would like to be elected president of the board and that all of them should vote for me. It was all set when the current president entered the room. He must have known that something fishy was going on. I continued in German with immediate translation by my friend, that I had to make an announcement and declared that

> "As the acting priest, I have to be a member of this board, and my priest will not allow a church board in which he isn't president. I, as acting pastor, will fill this position. Gentlemen, I request an immediate vote for who should be the president of the church board. I urge you to elect unanimously the priest, whose position then I will fill temporarily."

I gave everybody paper and pencil, and asked everyone "Please note who you would like to see president," and placed my own vote, too. After the votes were counted, all but the one who spoke in church this morning, voted for the priest. I accepted the chair position temporarily in lieu of the pastor. Immediately, and not unexpectedly, the good man resigned from his chair position and left the room.

"Well, we got rid of him now," I said in German, and showed the members the books just like I did this morning in the archbishop's office. The next Sunday I gave a full report in front of the assembled congregation. The next day, the secretary of the church board, my Pennsylvanian friend, informed the archbishop in writing that Mr. "So-and-So" had resigned from his position and that I was elected chairman of the board until the return of the pastor. The order of events wasn't quite accurately reported, but still, it was the truth.

Now we could work together without any distractions and that's just what we did. First of all I moved into a new room under the portal of the new house. We simply put up curtains that I could sleep in the open air and at the same time could receive members of my congregation properly. But one night it rained so hard through the curtains that I disassembled my bed and slept in the unfinished new house. This gave me the idea to continue the construction far enough, that one could actually live in the building. Since there was no money for the construction, the church board helped and explained to me the American way of making money. All the time the priest was in France, we tried everything to collect money to continue construction.

The day I saw for the first time the De Vargas procession in Santa Fe, the women of Guadalupe gave a great dinner which was given at Loretto Hall. We netted a profit of more than four hundred dollars. The De Vargas procession or more accurately, the performance of De Vargas's arrival in Santa Fe, impressed me more the first time I saw it than it does now. The procession was an accurate performance of the Spanish occupation of Santa Fe through General De Vargas in 1692. The reenactment is performed in Santa Fe every year but except for the cleric-historical interpretation the spectacle appears somewhat touristy, particularly in more recent years.

When the priest returned finally from France, a homecoming parade was held in his honor to show the appreciation of his congregation. He was very surprised when I led him through the new house. Five rooms were finished, even electric light was available, and construction of dining room and kitchen were advanced enough to be used. Dinner in his honor was served in my old room. After the priest poured himself a glass of wine and tasted it, he made a sour face, looked disapprovingly at me, and asked:

"What kind of wine did you buy?"

"I haven't bought it at all; I haven't touched your wine at all during your absence."

"You always kept the barrel closed?"

"Certainly not, or else the wine would have gone bad!" I responded in earnest.

"Germans don't know much about wine, all they know is beer," he said and informed me of my mistake. All the wine turned into vinegar, but this was about my biggest mistake during his absence. He was very satisfied with the situation he found after his return from France. Now he wanted to finish the house, which meant we had to find more money.

I thought of performing theater plays. Immediately I called upon all the young people and on 12 December we gave our first performance in the new hall upstairs. A staircase led from the hallway of the house to the upstairs quarters. (A fire escape from the highest window down was built as well on the outside which looked funny but, I suppose, was necessary for safety reasons.) I rehearsed with the young boys the Spanish Christmas play Los Pastores or the herders. Ten days before Christmas we started to give one performance per evening. Initially attendance was small, but increased once word spread in the community. One evening we even asked for one dollar cover charge from the Americans. After that performance some photographs were taken and the next day I took the entire group into town for a photo session. These pictures are still making the round among the pastores or herders.

My priest gave me the honor to arrange all the Christmas celebrations. Why he decided to go to the missions to celebrate Christmas, I have never understood. It was supposed to be his duty to be at the church, but gave me preference in managing the events; no other priest has ever done that. Still, I embarrassed myself. Lots of preparations for Christmas kept me so busy I haven't had enough time to prepare the service in English and Spanish well. Everything began well, but when I was going to hold the sermon I noticed that I forgot the small sheet of paper with my notes.

I always prepared my services well enough not to get stuck and therefore never had to read the sermon. The notes were always just a reassurance. It is not that easy to read midnight mass when the spirit is not quit so alert and the thoughts are slow. At first, I was scared to death when I noticed I forgot my notes, but I had to preach. Initially it went all right, but halfway through the English sermon, some people started to laugh. When I turned red and said a few more words, more people joined the commotion. The escalating laughter was my sign to think about an ending or else I had the entire congregation laughing.

It is easy in the English language to give words a different meaning; false pronunciation itself can do that. When more people began to smirk I was done with my patience and my sermon. I said immediately "Amen," made the cross, and I thought that I don't need these assaults. I stood there motionless for a moment and then said loud:

> My dear children, I am just a short time in this country and it is not easy to learn two foreign languages at the same time. You had your fun at my expense, which I think is not very polite. I could make fun of you in a second if I were to preach in German. Remember that after mass the worship of the Christ child is held. I will stand next to the cradle and hold the child in my arms when you come to pray. I will see what everybody will drop into the collection plate. Those who laughed will probably give the least. Now, I wish all of you a Merry Christmas and hope that you will make my Christmas celebration a bit more joyful than you did my Christmas mass.

This speech worked well as the collection plate was full. This was also the last collection I accepted in the Church of Guadalupe. Two or three days later, I received notice to come to the Cathedral as chaplain. I started my new position on 1 January [1913].

Father Küppers was assigned to Our Lady of Guadalupe Church until the end of 1912 before returning to the Cathedral. Courtesy Palace of the Governors Photo Archives (NMHM/DCA), #61357.

I did not like that change at all, but remembered well the time when I begged the archbishop to keep me as chaplain in the Cathedral. Now I had to go because obedience is the first order. Weeks later I learned that my former church board members came to see the Archbishop and requested my stay at the Church of Guadalupe. Naturally they were unsuccessful and left the Archbishop under unpleasant circumstances. I was disappointed and moved without trumpets and fanfare into the Cathedral. That's how the Catholic Church operates but that is all right. Were I poetically inclined I would create a nice poem about the Church of Guadalupe, its noble priest, and the pleasant people who remain my friends to this day.

At the Cathedral

Quite often one feels like a fish out of water, particularly when one is handed a surprise. I was very sorry to start my new position, and so were the people since they sent a delegation from the parish to Archbishop Pitaval requesting that I remain at the Guadalupe Church. As thankful as I truly was to the delegation, they were not received well. I never learned what the Archbishop told them about me—if he was happy or not with my work.

The one evidence of my good work came from my priest at the Guadalupe Church: "Here's the key to the presbytery and you may stop by anytime you want. You should visit every day, and if I am out, you have a key to my sacristy. You know where everything is, because you won't get as good a meal anywhere as you do here." This was a noble recognition of my services and I must say I still think back fondly of my days at the Guadalupe Church.

I noticed at the cathedral that every Saturday or before every feast day many folks from the Guadalupe Church came to have their confessions taken by me. And before leaving the confessional they took the liberty to ask me with a winning smile—of course in Spanish: "Como le va, Padrecito?"—"How are you, my dear pastor?" And that's how I knew that they were from my old congregation.

At the cathedral a new segment of my life began under the direction of my good friend Msgr. Fourchegu, who most graciously welcomed me as his new chaplain. I somehow suspect that the good priest was actively involved in my transfer. There is hardly any other priest in Santa Fe who contributed so much to the development of the town—if one could call it that at the time—than Monsignor Fourchegu, a highly pious man. Toward the end of 1912, he had built a new and long overdue presbytery. The second floor of the old building where he and his two chaplains roomed was dangerously instable. The floor could have collapsed at any moment, and in order to live there, one had to have a pure conscience and a decent life insurance.

Whether it was pure luck or not, I was very happy when Msgr. Fourchegu assigned me a room in the new presbytery. Thus, I was the first to reside in the spacious home. As new rooms were completed in the house, the other gentlemen relocated, one after another, until lastly the pastor himself moved in. Now the priests could enjoy some amenities; I, for one, did not have to go outside in the rain with an umbrella.[1]

My fellow chaplain at the Cathedral was a native of Switzerland. He was First chaplain and I, then, Second chaplain. He was the one who almost ruined my first Christmas in Santa Fe. We became good friends but he always treated me as his assistant which occasionally got on my nerves. It must have been the second evening since arriving at the Cathedral, during supper, when Archbishop Pitaval came to the presbytery and announced that there will be a short meeting after supper. There were four of us: the Archbishop, the Vicar General, and us two chaplains. The Archbishop assigned us chaplains our duties. I was to cover the missions, six of them, and was responsible for all sick calls. Only if I was indisposed, would the other chaplain have to go. The Indian School of St. Catherine as his main task was assigned to the First chaplain. The daily work and work assignments in the Cathedral were the responsibility of the Vicar General, to whom we reported.

The remaining task covered the parish school. We all expected to see responsibility for the parish school go to the Vicar General. Not only did he administer the building, but as priest it would have been his duty. However, to my great surprise and dismay, I was ordered to manage to the parish school. As long as the Sisters were good teachers, this isn't such a big deal, but there are always problems that require the attention of a seasoned priest. I did not like this assignment and I could tell that the Vicar General himself did not agree but put a good face on this decision.

If the priest had had my temper, the situation would have developed differently. But he didn't and I decided on a plan that I would implement the following morning. Shortly after breakfast I went to see the priest and put my cards on the table. The priest quickly responded that we want to follow the Archbishop's orders.

"Certainly, we have to do that, otherwise we'll be in trouble," I replied, "but the two of us could agree how to work together."

The old gentleman liked this idea and after we finished our discussion, the work plan was as follows:

Religious education had to be done by both chaplains under the supervision of the priest. The priest could attend classes as often as he wanted and whenever he felt like it. I was to see to it that the children would attend school regularly. The priest has control over the monies. Everything was under the supervision of the priest—as it should be.

Now I had plenty of credit with the priest, even more so than before. He overlooked that I went now and then, actually almost every day, to town for visits. I still have to point out: Every time I went to visit someone, I went to the Monsignor [Fourchegu] to let him know where I went and how to reach me. This, too, pleased him immensely, with the consequence that I could leave whenever I had a spare moment. Naturally, all my friends lived in the Guadalupe neighborhood and I used every opportunity to visit and to keep these friendships alive. Since I made new friendships quickly, it did not take long before I felt at home again at the Cathedral, just as I felt at home in the Guadalupe Church.

The cook's work began at seven in the morning until just after noon and then again from four o'clock until after dinner. She was never available at night, and also not in the afternoons from 1pm-4pm. I don't want to comment about her good cooking qualities because she was always courteous toward me. Once I explained to her that I did not have a healthy stomach and that the food did not agree with me, if it isn't prepared well. Apparently my concerns didn't help much since breakfast was the same every morning: a cup of coffee, a fried egg, sugar, bread and butter. What I wanted was variety.

Now and then I was able to say mass for the Loretto Sisters in the convent, and after mass there was a good breakfast. I enjoyed that immensely. Dear Sister Gertrud was in charge of the sacristy and was permitted to serve me breakfast. She soon figured out what I liked most. All too often I was reminded of my very first breakfast in New York, and here now I had the opportunity to have such a breakfast again. As soon as Sister Gertrud knew what I liked, there always was a big beefsteak with fried potatoes, along with fruit, fine coffee with milk or even cream and sugar ready for breakfast on the days I said mass in the convent. What I could never instill in her, however, was my desire for crêpes.

Once, when I had a craving for crêpes, I played a trick on the good sister. After mass I went to the study where breakfast was served and only took a cup of coffee. When the Sister brought the beefsteak, I shook my head and said: "My stomach doesn't feel well this morning." Then, she shook her head and felt sorry for me. When I came again one morning to the convent and was about to have breakfast there, I again would have liked to have crêpes. Naturally, it was again, beefsteak. The sister laughed mischievously when she placed the beefsteak in front of me and I was again about to apologize for an upset stomach.

"I suppose you'd rather go to 105 Guadalupe Street," she said, "where you can have crêpes for breakfast."

"Who told you that?" I asked surprised.

I was caught, but whenever I had wanted crêpes before, I went to the Guadalupe Church, much to the disappointment of dear Sister Gertrud. We remained friends and when I see her now and then in Santa Fe, I am always reminded of crêpes and her well prepared beefsteaks. By now, she is old and deaf, but a soul beyond reproach—a Spanish, neo-Mexican Sister, a child of this native soil.

The point here is not to criticize the meals at the Cathedral. All I am saying here is that meals come in different forms, depending on the availability of money or on the stomach that can take it. Monsignor Fourchegu never complained about the meals and I often admired him for his appetite, there was nothing that he could not eat.

For lunches the cook and I came to an agreement. Every day about thirty minutes before lunch was served she knocked at my door to tell me quickly what's for lunch. If it seemed something that my stomach could survive, I stayed for lunch. If not, I generally went to a restaurant where I could eat something for a few cents.

And since it wasn't likely for a priest to return from the missions before lunch, one had to eat out or remain hungry. When one returned late from the missions, only left-overs remained: cold potatoes, cold meat and beans, and cold coffee, and if one did not want to eat it, one had to go elsewhere. Today many would complain, but I did not dare to do so then.

Chaplains did not earn much money. The income of a chaplain at the Cathedral was twenty dollars a month and not a cent more. I remember many chaplains received only ten dollars—but then again every chaplain had free room and board. Since a chaplain did not receive much money from other sources, the picture was dim.

Thus it was difficult for each chaplain at the Cathedral to buy his own horse and buggy and maintain them. The priest was also responsible for alfalfa and hay for the horse. Generally, I had a sack of corn or oats in my room, and every day I gave some of it to my Navajo pony to make sure it was always well fed. This was the responsibility of the horse owner. The one who had a well fed horse showed that he loved his horse. A chaplain had to pay $150.00 for a horse and buggy which was seven months of salary. Nobody even thought of buying an automobile, but today just about everybody has one.

But those days were the good ol' days, and I remember them fondly. Discontent was not known then; and we had a good share of humor. If something did not work out the first time, it went better the second time. It goes without saying that a chaplain had to work hard, and it was not uncommon to be in a saddle or a buggy all day. When the day came to visit a mission, the horse was saddled or the buggy hitched, and off one went. It did not matter if the weather was nice or bad, rain or shine or snow and excuses were not acceptable since the elder priests had endured such strains for years.

I remember one afternoon I was going to go to Rio del Medio, nine miles from Santa Fe, for one of my regular visits. Horse and buggy were ready to go when a big thunderstorm rolled in. I tied down the horse in the yard and ran into the house to wait for the passing of the storm. But the weather just did not want to pass and I still had to drive nine miles to Rio del Medio to hold mass the next morning. Finally I decided to call off this visit and went to see the priest to tell him about my decision. "Good thinking," he responded, "then I will go myself." Moments later, I was back in the rain in my buggy, whisked the whip and passed the presbytery on my way to Rio del Medio, where I arrived in the end safely.

Here I remember an event that happened in March of last year [1930s]. My chaplain, who just started his job a month earlier, and I had been to Albuquerque. When we arrived late that evening in Embudo where one of my missions was, a sick call came from the Protestant hospital in Dixon, and simultaneously a sick child was brought in for his baptismal; and if that wasn't enough, a businessman from Santa Fe wanted to see me. I told the businessman right away to wait since there were more pressing tasks to be done. I then asked my chaplain "Would you mind going to the hospital, which is only half a mile away, and administer to the sick man?" He looked at me and quickly responded: "I don't feel like visiting a sick man just now." "Well then I'll go myself," I responded and went, while he remained calmly seated. When I returned from the hospital, my chaplain was gone. One of my parishioners came for him from Peñasco with a car to take him home. I, on the other hand, stayed at the mission since I also had to baptize the sick child. That's how it works now in this world: one has the wallet, the other one the money.[2]

Memories, of which I am particularly fond to this day, are those of teaching. I've done nothing in Santa Fe but teach one hour of religion and, when my hour was up, I left as quickly as possible. Generally I left the teaching to the priest just as it should be and as he liked it. The only dealings I had with school children were when in mornings, around 9 o'clock, one of the Sisters sent a list of absent children. If the list was long, which it usually wasn't, I went out and picked up the boys. In addition, the city's truant officer and I had an agreement that if he catches one of my boys in the street, he was to take them to my school, and if I found kids from the public schools in the street, I was to take them to their school. But this was only an agreement, and neither one of us bothered about the affairs of the other.

One day the priest complained that the parents of the school children are not paying enough tuition and that it was almost impossible to continue to operate the school under such circumstances. Once a month at the Cathedral, I believe it was the first Sunday, a collection for the school was requested, but it didn't bring much. At some point, I decided to do something about it. One Sunday I said the 9 o'clock Mass for the Americans or Anglos in English. And after all my research about this issue, I said something like the following:

> It appears to me, that it is unnecessary to announce God's word, for the reason that you think the church has to give everything to you and you don't have to give anything in return. Look at your children. They are not attending our school; and those of you, who, indeed, have their children go to our school, are not happy; even complain about having to pay tuition. Every Sunday, we are holding a collection for the school, but few of you are giving anything worthwhile. Now we want to make this short: I will come down from the pulpit and hold a collection myself and I expect that every church member will contribute something to the maintenance of the school. From today on, every time I am holding or attending mass, we will do this, because we cannot go on like this."

Then I stepped down from the pulpit. The priest, who was sitting in the Sanctorum, looked at me with surprise—but friendly enough, that I felt good. So I passed over three Sunday collectors who must have felt slighted, took the collection bag and made slowly the round from one person to the next. I had to smile frequently, because almost every one put something into the bag. Some of the Americans did not want to look cheap and so quite a few dollars were collected. After mass I gave the collection to my priest. A Sunday collection brings generally five dollars or so, but this time the bag held ten times that much. I did the same at High Mass with similar success. My priest was very pleased. When I did no longer have to hold mass anymore, he predicted, that the collections would now be as meager again as in the past. [But he was wrong]; the priest remained happy and other things did not bother me.

The work on the missions wasn't all that bad. I was used to traveling 60 and 70 miles in the buggy although the mission farthest away that still belonged to the Cathedral, La Cienega, was only 15 miles away. The mission, second-farthest away, was already mentioned, Rio del Medio.

To read mass in Tesuque, one drove six miles from Santa Fe. After mass, I spent time with a German family and the lady of the house was an excellent cook. Whenever I came to visit she tried to outdo herself and provided me with a particularly good meal. It was the family of Alfons Dockweiler who accumulated a fortune growing fruits and vegetables. Well rested and fed, I continued my trip to Rio del Medio after lunch.

My predecessor was a chaplain who made this trip on foot, walking four or five miles to Rio del Medio, but this did not suit me. First, I tried the buggy, but too often I had to get out and lead the horse and buggy along dangerous and steep ravines. Then I tried the horse. Yet, on horseback too, it was so dangerous that I had to dismount and guide the horse along the ravines. Only a mule would have been sure-footed enough for these steep paths. Since I did not own a mule, I had the bright idea to rent a small burro because burros go slowly but safely along all the cliffs and ravines. For my third trip, after another splendid lunch in the house of my German hostess, I mounted a small burro.

In my left hand I held my little case with the communion wine and other necessities and with my right hand I held the small stick to direct the burro. A burro will not tolerate a bridle and can't be guided with one. Well, the trip went well and I did not have to dismount once. This is proof that a burro, and a sure-footed one at that, can navigate slowly and with stoic calm the cliffs—and rough paths of life. Everything would have gone just fine, had it not been for some modern invention, totally unknown to the burro.

The next day, my burro, in whom I now had complete confidence, and I were on our way back from Rio del Medio and then going directly to Tesuque. As we unhurriedly went along, my burro must have been spooked by a roaring sound because he leaped to the side and I almost fell off. Then I noticed what was happening: "Honk, honk"—an automobile approached us from behind and likely it wasn't a new one with that noisy spectacle surrounding it. My burro lost its entire cool and ran as fast as its short legs allowed, off the street and into the fields. I dropped my case and, holding on to the animal's neck, I tried to control it with my stick as best as I could. But nothing could deter the burro and he ran until I fell off. I never saw the burro again. The moral here is, that it is dangerous to trust an ass as it makes you look like an ass [fool].

The hardest, but also the most gratifying tasks were the many sick calls at the Cathedral. I have to say that when a sick call came in, no matter how far, within five minutes I was on my horse and on my way.

This reminds me of some interesting stories. One evening, I came home late from a sick call and was very tired. After a cold and stale supper I went to bed. I must have fallen into a deep sleep as I did not hear the door bell ring in my room. Suddenly somebody stood next to my bed, shaking me so firmly, that I woke up rather stunned. I recognized the fellow; it was the first chaplain, who angrily yelled at me: "Didn't you hear your bell? It's been ringing now for about half an hour. There's a sick call and it is your duty to go." Once I comprehended the situation, I told him "I know it is my duty and will go," and asked him to get out. I quickly put on my robe and opened the door to the house, where a young woman asked me to see her dying father immediately. I was ready by the time the doctor from the near-by hospital, whom she had called, passed by to take me along. By the time we arrived at the house of the dying man, he was dead. I was very sorry—a stroke had put an end to his life. After I recited prayers for the deceased, I consoled the family and eventually asked the young woman who called on me: "How long did you ring the bell at the Sacristy"?

"About half an hour" was her response.

"Whom did you call first?"

"The first chaplain" she replied.

"And then?" I asked.

"Then I called on you, but you didn't respond either."

"And then you rang the first chaplain's bell again?"

"Yes," she responded, "and he came and first of all, shouted at me that it was your duty to go and not his."

One may think about this case which ever way it pleases.

In another case, I returned home at about ten o'clock in the morning after finishing some business in town. My colleague approached me instantly to let me know that a sick call was waiting for me. Since it was only a ten-minute horseback ride, I left immediately. The sick man was dead by the time I arrived. My colleague, instead of going himself, waited until I came back. Again, one may think about this case whatever one wants.

One afternoon while taking confessions, my priest came to tell me that a sick woman was waiting for me in La Cañada, some eight miles from Santa Fe. I left the confessional immediately, took my buggy and departed. On my way I noticed that a small cloud was turning into a bigger, darker cloud and I pushed my horse to go faster. When I arrived at the sick woman's house the first heavy rain drops were coming down and soon a heavy thunderstorm was unloading its weight. The storm hovered for a long time and it was getting dark already. Since it was Saturday and I had duties to perform Sunday morning, I decided to return home. It was already dark when I pulled up at an arroyo or a ditch and the rushing noise of water indicated the danger in crossing it.

My first thought was to turn around, but when a priest is missing at the Cathedral no mass would be read on Sunday! I spurred on my faithful horse and off we went into the raging river—I was already wet from top to bottom and couldn't get any more wet. How I arrived on the other side, I still don't know to this day. I only felt the current and the swaying buggy in it. Since the force of the water floated us down river and I did not know where we were, I just left it up to my horse to get us home. A second thunderstorm broke over us, but finally after two hours in torrid rain under thunder and lightning, we arrived in Santa Fe.

It was ten o'clock at night. I knew I wouldn't find any dinner at the Cathedral, so I decided to go to Guadalupe Street knowing I'd be warmly welcomed. I tied down my horse, stroke its mane, and ran into the house where I would receive help. I stopped at the house of my former neighbor at Guadalupe Church who has passed away but back then helped me improve my English language sermons.

Her daughter was now living alone in the house. She was a teacher in her sixteenth year in the Santa Fe public schools and a well-respected and capable person. When I knocked at her door dripping wet and announcing myself, she opened immediately. A warm cup of coffee with a good additive [likely a shot of liquor] did wonders to get me back on track. A younger neighbor let me borrow all the necessary clothing, so that I was soon back in dry clothes again. Dinner made me feel human again. Just before midnight, I drove up at the Cathedral, where I first tended to my horse and then went to bed.

The next morning it was again raining cats and dogs but since I had the first mass at the Cathedral I could not accept any sick calls and thus was lucky to stay out of the rain. I was supposed to read the second mass as well but about half an hour before mass I received another sick call—one that could not wait another minute. It wasn't very far from the Cathedral but it needed a horse to get there. Should I go and make the visit or should I send my colleague? I was about to go hold second mass while my colleague had enough time until his mass, the last one, started.

I went to his room and saw that he just got out of bed! I told him about the urgent call and firmly told him "I will ride out to the sick man, but if I am not back in time for mass, you will have to do mine—and your own! I can't make this sick call and then do the last mass—I am only human." I had never before spoken so forcefully to my colleague. But the decision was made, and, on top of it, I planned to play joke on him.

I went to the kitchen and asked: "May I have two good cups of coffee?" Seeing the concerned expression on the Mexican woman's face I added: "Please don't tell anyone, I'll explain later." The two cups of coffee felt good. Afterward I stepped fearlessly out into the heavy rain. When one is warm enough on the inside one does not have to fear catching any illness. Then I galloped quickly to see the sick man and arrived there in time.

But now the spiel began: I needed to ride back slowly so not to arrive there before mass started—and since I had already broken the rule of fasting I couldn't say mass anyway. I slowly mounted my horse and, in heavy rain, rode slowly back to the Cathedral. I heard the bells ringing and was happy to have been able to stick it to my colleague who now not only had to say mass and give the sermon, but had to do it twice.

I returned so unhurriedly that some of the late churchgoers who saw me looked surprised, especially since it was raining so miserably. When I arrived at the Cathedral, I took care of my horse, and then went to the kitchen to have breakfast. I gave the cook some vague explanation, just enough to not alert her. Then I disappeared for the remainder of the morning in my room and enjoyed a few hours of solitude.

Once, one of those tricks almost blew up in my face. One morning I was to officiate a funeral at the cathedral and I was to accept the body at eight o'clock at the church entrance. That morning, however, I had for some reasons stomach cramps but I was still ready at 8 o'clock waiting in the sacristy. Nobody came and I was waiting for half an hour and then some more time. Had I been able to take some medicine I would have been fine, but this way, I could barely stand. Partially out of desperation, I started mass thinking that when the people arrive with the body they could bring it into the church without my help.

Everything went fine until I just finished the offering. That's when unfortunately the Archbishop came from the sacristy to the church. I must have turned red all over my face, because he looked rather surprised at me, and quickly left the church. It wasn't two minutes later, that Monsignor Fourchegu came in rather angrily, stepped up to the alter and bellowed: "What are you doing? You are saying mass without anybody attending? Stop immediately and wait until the corpse arrives—I will receive them!" I remained motionless at the altar when finally the funeral procession arrived.

The priest received the corpse, said a few words directed toward my disobedience, and then I was able to continue mass. After mass, the priest himself went to the grave to bury the body. The time until Monsignor Fourchegu returned felt like an eternity because I feared the justifiable penalty. As soon as I heard his steps in the hallway, I followed him into his room, knelt down in front of him and asked for his forgiveness. I got a stern lecture which I still remember to this day, but when I left his room everything felt fine. In the afternoon the archbishop came to visit, opened the door to my room, and there I was given another reprimand—and all without any sympathy for my stomach. I just had to swallow and digest the two rebukes. I felt better after this was all over.

As priest I was a figure of authority, and still, at heart I also felt like being a young fellow. It was my greatest pleasure to gather young men around me to play and have fun, and also to provide serious entertainment, even to offer deep philosophical instructions. Thus, I gathered a few young men and founded a so-called Club. I don't want to bore anyone with what I told the boys and what I taught them, but I do want to explain how I kept their interest alive.

While I tried to spend time with the boys during the week, every Sunday afternoon—save for any emergency—was earmarked for us. And twice we brought excitement into this little town of Santa Fe. One Sunday we gathered in front of the Cathedral to go on a rabbit hunt in the fields outside of downtown since, obviously there weren't any rabbits in downtown Santa Fe—at least not the kind that you can beat to death with a club.

Equipped with big clubs and a whistle, our troop marched singing and yodeling through town. That hadn't happened before in Santa Fe, but the more people opened their windows and the more people came out of their houses to see what's going on, the louder we sang. We passed Sunmount Sanatorium silently, as there were no rabbits of any kind—only the finest and well educated people lived there. We arrived on the property of a fine, old German immigrant—Mr. Nagel. He owned 400 acres of land in the foothills and there we could let off steam to our hearts' content. Crisscrossing these mountains and seeing these rabbits run away, tails between their hind legs, made me think that humans, whose conscience wasn't pure, also take their tail between their legs and run when a situation grows difficult.

Yet another time we had a different thought on how to get the attention of Santa Fe's bourgeois citizens. Again on a Sunday afternoon we gathered in front of the Cathedral. All the boys came on burros, only I came on horseback. The biggest burro led our procession and the entire cavalcade followed. There were about forty of us, each on his burro, all riding through town—with me taking the end on my tall horse. One does not see these kinds of events anymore today. It is more fashionable nowadays to visit movie theaters or cruising in automobiles or, even worse, hanging out with girls. The burros then were not stupid but knew morals and etiquettes.

Another hobby of mine was construction and I once had a small opportunity to build something. I always enjoyed visiting a chapel that looked neat and clean inside. I did not like seeing a chapel whose interior needed renovation after every serious rain fall. Such a chapel was in Tesuque, some seven miles outside of Santa Fe. It simply needed a new roof.

At the time I did not know much about the Santa Fe style as it is known today, which became popular when writers and painters started to settle in New Mexico. Before then everything was built in the Mexican style, a deviation from the Spanish style and yet still independent at the same time.

If New Mexico were to pass laws that require Spanish Americans to construct their home in Mexican style, the state would look even prettier than it already does. But I was then as ignorant as most Anglo Americans and not yet comfortable with traditional Mexican architecture. When the little church in Tesuque needed a new roof, my heart was in the right place but not my brains. I started begging for money to put a new roof on the church—with a steeple roof among all these Mexican style homes. I organized the people of Tesuque, and we did everything ourselves.

Every morning I went with horse and buggy from Santa Fe to Tesuque to be there by eight in the morning and within two weeks we had the steeple roof on the chapel. And every time I happen to see the steeple roof in the far distance, I get angry about my stupidity. (Perhaps when I am even older, I might get angry about other things as well, and perhaps even about the idea of writing down my memoirs).

When I was chaplain in Santa Fe, I did not always stay at home waiting for people to visit me. No, I went out to visit folks, particularly Anglo Americans as they were generally known for not attending religious services. And one couldn't entirely blame them: except for the liturgical ceremonies in church, everything was in Spanish, which obviously was Greek to most of them.

Once I was called to visit a sick man who was highly affected by some wasting disease. He was Irish, had married outside the church, and had neglected all his religious obligations. His excuse was that he hadn't heard an English language service in years. On another occasion, I learned that a traveler passing through Santa Fe fell ill in a hotel whose owner wasn't particularly friendly toward Catholics. The poor guy was in a small room on the third floor of the hotel, and when he suddenly saw a priest next to his bedside, who could at least speak English, he was so surprised.

He exclaimed: "I didn't think priests spoke English here."

"Well," I said, "the priests are just about the only ones who speak English and can master the Spanish language as well."

Yet another case was an old friend, Mike Stanton; he is dead now. I did not know, and I think none of us priests knew, that Mike was catholic. I remember well the times I was called to visit Mike. I went there a few times, and we became friends. And the only reason he neglected his religious duties, was that everything was in Spanish. He was glad he had a priest nearby until his spirit left his earthly skin. That is why I had to find those local Americans who did not attend church anymore.

I had a good friend in Santa Fe, who moved here with his family from Illinois for health reasons. He was German and I spent hours with him. All day he sat the veranda in front of his house, and we touched on many things during our conversations; I learned a lot about America from him. During our conversations we discussed the need for organizations which might be beneficial and necessary to the church. Eventually we had the idea to organize Catholic men and start up a Catholic social club. I knew this was a needed organization.

Another issue was of great concern to me. In the Catholic Church it is required to obey the rules of Easter and I knew of several good standing Americans who forgot about this obligation. The closer the end of Lent was in sight and the less I saw certain gentlemen, the more I was on their case. I went from one office to the next, introduced myself, and in my ignorance often thought that everybody was Catholic—at least in Santa Fe. So in the City of the Holy Faith I read them the riot act because they did not show up in church on Sundays and even worse, did not follow their obligations during Easter.

Sometimes I was ridiculed, once even thrown out, but I learned that house calls were necessary if one expects to do the church's spiritual work. Too often I was told, "I don't have the time during the day and can only visit the confessional in the evenings."

"Fine," I replied, "then I'll take your confession tonight in my room, or I'll be in church early—very early—in the morning waiting for you and you won't loose any time."

All this gave me food for thought and I really tried to gather the men. I drafted and printed a handbill for all men in Santa Fe asking them to join the German-Roman Central Club of St. Louis. Then I proudly took the 500 copies to my room and left them on the table. Unfortunately, when one is not particularly clever it is difficult to develop smarts. Think of it: what impression would I make on the Irish Catholics and even worse, the Spanish Catholics when asking them to join the German-Roman Central Club? I was saved from distributing the leaflets and, subsequently, from the embarrassment.

The good Father Derache from the Sanatorium was visiting me that afternoon, saw the leaflets, and read a copy. Without hesitation [and without Küppers noticing it] he took all the copies and gave a copy to my priest. I hadn't mentioned a word to him, since I wanted to present him with a fait accomplis. When I returned home later that evening, I could not find my printed material. At dinner I didn't mention anything [about the missing leaflets], but noticed my priest to be in a good mood.

In order to not humiliate myself further and to ascertain what was known, I went to see Father Derache after dinner. He offered me a pinch of snuff and then started to laugh. I figured I embarrassed myself thoroughly, and owed my priest an apology for not having kept him in the loop. I was wrong, and just before going to bed, went straight to his room, offered my apologies with the excuse of inexperience. He contemplated for a while nodding his head and suggested I form a chapter of the Knights of Columbus. The final word was spoken and with the help of Father Fourchegu I began to organize a chapter of the Knights of Columbus in Santa Fe.

There were already a few members of the Knights of Columbus in Santa Fe, but I didn't understand their structure at all. And when I inquired about it, I only received forgiving looks as if saying "you poor fool, you'll have yet a lot to learn." It was sufficient for me that this organization was one of the largest for men and that my priest wanted to see one formed in Santa Fe—although, he once told me not to mention the idea to the Archbishop [Pitaval]. I could not imagine, though, why the archbishop might object.

So I looked little by little for all the Anglo and Hispanic Americans that appeared to be suited for such an organization and at the same time developed the application forms, which I submitted to my priest for review. After I had gathered enough applicants, the few Santa Fe members of the Knights of Columbus who belonged to the admissions committee, came together and prepared the necessary steps for initiation. The priest, however, slowed the process for inexplicable reasons until the archbishop was traveling to the East. Then he encouraged me to get everything organized as quickly as possible.

Archbishop Pitaval did not look kindly upon the Knights of Columbus and words about the Santa Fe Council, which appeared in 1913, alluded to that:

> [Original in English] Santa Fe Council No. 1707, located at Santa Fe N.M., etc.—was organized on the 19th day of October 1913—. This council should have been organized years previous, but circumstances which is [sic] best not to mention here prevented it until this time.

Under enormous pressure we worked hard to get everything ready before Archbishop Pitaval's return. Even telegrams were sent to New Haven, Connecticut, headquarter of the Knights of Columbus, to receive all the permits in time. One organizational meeting after another was held during that period in Santa Fe, as the following excerpts from the New Mexican show:

> [Original in English] K.Of C.Meet Tonight—The K. of C. and the proposed new members will meet at 7:30 o'clock tonight in Fireman's hall on San Francisco Street and a large attendance is desired as matters of great importance are coming up. The prospects of establishing a strong council in Santa Fe are considered exceedingly bright owing to the untiring efforts of the Rev. P. Küppers. Some of the most prominent Catholics in the City have applied for membership in the council to be established.

After the council in Santa Fe became a fact, the New Mexican commented:

> Following the efforts of Father Küppers, assistant priest of the Cathedral of St. Francis, a Knight of Columbus Council has been formed.

On the day of the inaugural ceremony, it was the first time in the history of Santa

Fe that Hispanic Americans and Anglo Americans, poor and rich, educated and uneducated, gathered in an organization that included all Americans. The 19th of October 1913 is a mile marker in the Catholic history of Santa Fe.

Santa Fe grew on me and I hated the thought of having to leave this little town. Even my ambitions to become a Priest have long been thrown by the wayside [just to stay in Santa Fe]. But all of a sudden the newspaper announced in a big headline:

> [Original in English] The Rev. Peter Küppers, assistant at the Cathedral of St. Francis, has been appointed by the archbishop the new pastor of the parish of Chaparito.
> Father Küppers succeeds Father Plantard, who resigned the pastorate of Chaparito recently owing to ill health and went to Las Vegas. The parish of Chaparito is a large one. The Church is 25 miles east of Las Vegas.
> On arriving in Santa Fe over a year ago, Father Küppers was given a position as assistant at Guadalupe Church, succeeding Father Hartmann. Later on he came to the Cathedral and has been very active in the cause of religion. He is well known in the city, especially with the younger men. It was through his effort that the local Council of the Knight of Columbus was formed here.

Well, now there you have it; but it wasn't quite that simple. After barely a year [in Santa Fe] I had to move again. And here is how it came about. One day I went to see the archbishop—and I should mention that we priests at the cathedral had the privilege to be on a more informal basis with him. Archbishop Pitaval, then, lived in the house on the grounds of the archdiocese garden which was known all over for its beauty.

The garden was laid out by the first archbishop, John Baptist Lamy, who had all the trees and bushes imported from France. In the garden is a spacious adobe home in which Archbishop Pitaval resided. The archbishop also had a so-called archiepiscopal palace, built by Archbishop [Jean Baptiste Lamy]. The palace was used rarely. When we priests from the Cathedral wanted to see the archbishop, we passed through the small parish garden and crossed an alley into the archiepiscopal garden.

If we needed to discuss something important with the archbishop, we went straight to the reception area in the archbishop's office and if we just wanted to make a visit, we went first into the kitchen to find out from Miss Robinson if the archbishop was busy. Since Miss Robinson served a good cup of coffee and a fine piece of cake, I liked visiting the archbishop's home and did so on many occasions, Archbishop Pitaval was always good to me and I had complete trust in him, so that I felt completely at home and considered him my mentor.

It was one December morning 1913 when I was going to see the archbishop. Upon passing the archiepiscopal palace on my way to the archbishop's residence, I heard voices in the palace. Alert to the voices, I only understood the words "I will send him to Chaparito," and I knew intuitively that this was meant for me, and returned quickly to my room. Indeed, it didn't take long when my priest entered my room and asked me to follow him to his room. There he told me with personal regrets that the archbishop was going to send me to Chaparito and that I should visit the archbishop immediately to receive my appointment as priest.

I was really pleased with this appointment, because it isn't easy to become a priest after only two years. Upon telling me the news, the archbishop added that

> "starting immediately, you're relieved from any duties at the Cathedral. Tomorrow you'll go to Las Vegas, from there you'll take the coach to Chaparito, where you'll check out the location and see how things are going."

"Just don't tell anybody yet," added the archbishop, "until I will appoint your successor."

Then something unexpected happened. During lunch at the Cathedral, a sick call came in. The priest asked me to see who was ringing the bell. And when I return shortly thereafter, I just said: "It's a sick call to Rio del Medio and the call appears urgent."

"Get ready," said the other chaplain.

"Well," I responded, "I am tired of this; I always have to go and now I am tired of answering sick calls, I won't go and that's it."

The priest looked at me with big eyes, but understood the joke. He replied: "I've been very pleased with your work here and now after almost a year on the job, you refuse to go? I know it is far."

"I'm tired, and I think the other one could make this call."

"What?" the first chaplain yelled, "I'll go right away to the archbishop and will report your refusal," and off he went.

The priest and I had tears in our eyes from laughing so hard, and went to our rooms to await the outcome of the chaplain's report. Fifteen minutes later, the chaplain returned, banged on my door, which I had locked in anticipation, and bellowed "I have enough for now; it is always the new ones that receive preferential treatment."

"Don't make such fuss over this," I said from behind the door, "it is better to obey the archbishop's order to go to Rio del Medio."

After my colleague left, the priest and I went together to see the archbishop and had another heartfelt laugh about this event. When my colleague returned from the sick call, he found a note to immediately see the archbishop. I could well imagine what had happened there, because my colleague came to my room and holding his hand out, said "Congratulations, you old fox."

The following day I went to Las Vegas to catch a ride to Chaparito. However, the outgoing priest, Father Gilberton, advised me not to continue my trip. The deep snow out on the plains would render any trip to Chaparito impossible, so that I took the next train back in a rather subdued mood.

The more I thought about all this, the less I liked my new postition as priest. The missions, I was told, are very strenuous and very far apart; the roads, particularly during the winter time, almost impassable; and the people live scattered all over on their farms that cannot provide enough water for their fields. In some places there isn't any clean drinking water.

At Christmas I was supposed to be in Chaparito and the closer the day of departure came, the more heartbreaking it became to leave my beloved Cathedral. I went to see the archbishop to tell him my concerns, and mentioned that since I didn't know how to cook, I would likely starve to death within a week or so.

He just laughed and finally said, "Just make sure to take along a good housekeeper from Santa Fe."

"Can you recommend one?" I asked.

He thought about it for a moment, and I think, he knew very well that the choice of a good housekeeper was the most important decision to be made, when one works on missions, particularly in New Mexico. Besides, the culinary well-being is an important factor for a priest who is traveling day in and day out, with horse and buggy. He should have decent meals, not just beans, chili, black coffee, and tortillas, upon returning home from the missions.

"Take Dona Maria along, who attended to your household already during your time at Guadalupe," said the archbishop.

She was a very good person and knew how to prepare a good meal; indeed, she was an excellent cook. But I wanted more than a cook. I didn't want to become bored; and while Spanish Americans are good people, Europeans have different expectations. Just like the American, the European wants to have an intelligent conversation. My idea was to find someone with whom it was possible to conduct an intellectual discussion. I told the archbishop accordingly, and he understood. After a moment of contemplation, he said

"Why don't you ask Mrs. "so and so;" her mother is dead, as you know, since you yourself buried her. Just ask her. You've tasted her cooking before, when you visited her for her crêpes."

"This is a good suggestion," I replied, "but she has a permanent job as a teacher with lots of experience."

"Perhaps she can teach in Chaparito, which would be quite some help for you and the missions?"

Said and done, and I took my chances in asking her. I must have applied all my powers of persuasion successfully, because after two or three days, my new housekeeper tendered her resignation as a teacher in Santa Fe to devote herself to the missionary work. Now I was reassured that I would have at least a decent meal after long travels to the missions. I've never been a friend of fancy gourmet meals, but a solid meal like Sauerkraut and pork had always been a winner with me. And I will continue to receive such meals.

During my time at the Cathedral, I don't remember having had any such meals. All in all, American food is far too opulent. With meals, more frugal and less wide-ranging, far less people would have appendicitis or stomach cancer.

The evening before my departure, it was the 22nd of December 1913 I received a big surprise which I will never forget. In cooperation with Monsignor Fourchegu, I worked hard for the Knights of Columbus. I made sure that they had a nicely furnished classroom in the parish for their gatherings. To avoid large expenses, I bought most of the furniture from the old DeVargas hotel, and with it outfitted the Knights of Columbus first home adequately. I also gave up a considerable portion of my personal library.

Now, rather unexpectedly, my presence was requested at the Knights of Columbus home. A big banquet was arranged for my farewell and afterwards so many speeches were given about my achievements in those two years that I became dizzy—and all I did was my duty. The high point of this evening was when the Grand Knight, as a sign of gratitude, presented me with a gilded chalice, which Archbishop Pitaval had consecrated earlier. This left such an impression on me, that I could only stammer a few words of appreciation.

After the gathering was over, three members of the Knights of Columbus accompanied me, each carrying as many of my presents as they possibly could—mostly tobacco and cigarettes. I, on the other hand, carried proudly my own personal chalice, which I have used ever since for the holy mass. The Santa Fe New Mexican wrote up the following:

> [Original in English] Knights Present Chaplain Küppers with Gold Chalice.
> Presenting their chaplain, Father Peter Küppers, with a gold chalice, beautifully engraved, the Knights of Columbus extended him their hearty wishes for success in his new field of labor.
> The announcement of the appointment of Father Küppers, for over a year assistant priest at the Cathedral, to be pastor at Chaparito, 25 miles east of Las Vegas, at first brought sorrow to the priest's many friends here, especially to the Knights of Columbus, whose Council he organized in Santa Fe. But realizing that the field of labor for the energetic pastor would be broader, the Knights felt satisfied at the honor bestowed on their chaplain etc.

Perhaps, based on the article, they were happy to see me leave after all. It is true, nobody is irreplaceable, regardless of how smart or dim-witted or conceited a person is. Truth to be told, the dumber a person, the more conceited he or she is.

To Chaparito

On the morning of 23 December 1913 I said good-bye to Archbishop Pitaval. I did not feel particularly well as I had a hunch of what lay ahead of me. My desire to become a priest was at a low point. In the two years that I spent in Santa Fe I made good friends whom I would dearly miss. Besides, I had a good idea of what life on an isolated mission post would be like. I had the audacity to beg the archbishop to keep me in Santa Fe and explained that I'd prefer the position of chaplain at the cathedral to the independence of the missions. But it didn't help, even tears came to the eyes—not the archbishop's, but mine—but to no avail. At the cathedral I bid good-bye to my pastor, a good man with a heart of gold. He gave me a portable altar as a good-bye present and pointed out: "To this day, no chaplain has ever received a gift from me, and whenever you use it, remember me."

Sadly, I left and went to the train station where my newly hired housekeeper already awaited me. Off we went by train to Las Vegas and the closer we came, the more it snowed. By the time we arrived in Las Vegas, there were two feet of snow. A car was supposed to take us from Las Vegas to Chaparito, about thirty miles across the plains. The priest who awaited us in Las Vegas shook his head, concerned about the risk of undertaking such a trip in this nasty weather. He told me that the only automobile available in the entire community of Chaparito was on its way.

I was scared to death when the little Lizzy drove up. Having a suspicion about the things to come, the priest put a bottle of whiskey in my overcoat. Six people were already waiting in the little Lizzy and now came the two of us along with my luggage. The thought immediately crossed my mind, that it was such a pity that my buggy and the two horses were not here with me now. I would have preferred my buggy, but the day before I had a man take it with the horses to Chaparito and wait for me there.

The Church at Chaparito, here pictured in 1913, was Father Küppers's first assignment outside of Santa Fe. Courtesty Palace of the Governors Photo Archives (NMHM/DCA), #119863.

Out into the plains, into the snowstorm, with no roads to see, slow driving, the little car was puffing and huffing. Unavoidably we got stuck, no backwards, no forwards, and then it was all over. Lizzy lost all her energy, caught a cold, and started to cough, and was unwilling to go any farther. There we were—stuck in deep snow and it was cold. I felt particularly sorry for a four-year-old child that accompanied us and suffered from consumption. The chauffeur couldn't do anything but trudge back to Las Vegas to find help. In the meantime, to avoid freezing to death, I suggested walking in the snow to the nearest farmhouse and awaiting help there. I took little Martina in my arms and we walked about a mile through deep, deep snow to the next house where a poor Spanish family pleasantly welcomed us.

Under a pretense I excused myself into a second room and took a long—very long—gulp from the bottle, because I knew about the conditions of my lungs. Then I secretly gave the girl a little sip and took another long swill for myself to get really warm. Then I quickly lit a big cigar to avoid being caught with liquor breath. After darkness, finally, another car arrived puffing and took us back to Las Vegas. The trip back was only six miles, but these were a very long six miles. We spent the night in a hotel. The next morning I tried to find somebody who would take us in a buggy to Chaparito, which was slower, but much safer. We rounded up a few good blankets and I took another gulp from the bottle. This is not a sin. The only irritation was my new housekeeper, who obviously had never been in a situation like that. But as years went by, she showed more stamina, bravery and trust in God than I did.

Finally the three of us—teamster, housekeeper and I—were on our way to Chaparito. It was the day before Christmas and midnight mass awaited me. What a trip this was—slowly through the snow and bitter cold, the teamster had to guess the road. Luckily, we had some good stuff along with us which we shared liberally to keep warm. The roads, as I learned later, were beyond any description. After dusk settled in, we saw a small chapel close to the road surrounded by so-called bonfires. Still three miles to Chaparito—endless three miles, so it seemed!

It was about nine o'clock at night when we arrived in Chaparito. Only a few houses could be made out, until we finally reached the plaza. Even in the dark, the village chapel made a friendly appearance. Near to the church stretched a long house, which I presumed was the rectory. We stopped and checked out the house. Nobody was there and we were about to freeze to death. I sent the driver off to find a human being, but when he did not return I broke a window. I climbed into the house and let my housekeeper in through the door. The inside of the house was so cold. I found a candle, an indication that I was in the right house, et fiat lux [and it turned light]. My next-door neighbor strolled by to see who broke into the rectory. Because he was such a faithful friend over the years, I will mention his name: Don Isidro, sacristan and companion of the priests of Chaparito. He did not look very trustworthy, especially for a Christmas evening, but then, I think we did not look all that much better. He checked me out critically and finally asked:

"Are you, then, the new priest? We expected you yesterday already."

"If you expected me, why didn't you start a fire? It would have warmed up the house a little. We are freezing."

"There is no wood stove," was his response, "only a tiled stove and there's a cooking stove in the kitchen."

I saw what was going on—my first real experience as a missionary. Only the bare necessities were available and not even those at times. Two beds were supposed to be here, but there was only one. I asked for some food, because we hadn't eaten all day and only took a sip from the bottle now and then to stay warm. My future sacristan disappeared only to return after a few minutes with black coffee, tepid, no sugar, no milk, and very strong. With it came a piece of cake whose contents I could not identify. It must have been something special since it was Christmas. When I asked where all the people were, he answered that they are all attending the Christmas dance in the community hall.

"At a dance—this starts out pretty dandy," I thought.

Then I told him: "Ring the bells at eleven to let the people know that there will be a midnight mass."

"Now, please go to the dance hall," I added, "and tell the people that the new pastor arrived and that we will celebrate midnight mass together. All people have to come to church."

"And when you return," I told him, "bring me a mattress and blankets, I would like to rest for an hour before I go to the church and prepare everything for mass." Everything was done as I requested.

I left the bed to my housekeeper. Not only did it seem the polite thing to do, it also appeared to me that nobody has slept in that bunk for over a year. I got comfortable on the mattress in my future office. Then I was ready for midnight mass, but I wasn't in too good a mood. I tried to explain to the people how Christ child must have felt that first Christmas night, and had he been as cold as I was, it must have been really bad. Eventually I asked the people to lend me two or three stoves and to find me a decent bed. I didn't say a word about Christmas lunch because my housekeeper came prepared: she had bought a turkey while we were staying in Las Vegas. When I was invited after mass by one of my new parishioners to have lunch with him and his family, I declined politely. I did not want to miss the turkey.

What else can I say? The first days were very cold, there was nothing in the house and I was lucky to have had at least ten dollars in cash. Next day my horses and buggy arrived and the man who chauffeured the team from Santa Fe to Chaparito requested ten dollars for his services—all my savings. The collection plate for Christmas mass held about two dollars.

On my second day in Chaparito I had quite a scare. An old cart pulled up in front of my house and eight to ten elderly but strong men climbed off the cart. They requested entry to the house. Each one introduced himself [a different draft identified the men as penitentes] and then they presented their request.

Pointing toward an old harmonium in my room, they said: "This belongs to our church in Los Torres and when the former priest closed down our church, he moved the harmonium to Chaparito."

"This is a good beginning," I thought, "but it was best not to tangle with these men." But it turned out over the years that they were the faithful ones of my parish.

"Well," I answered meekly, "if the harmonium belongs to the church in Los Torres, then take it right away with you, and if the church is closed, just reopen it again, because I will come soon and read mass. Just return cheerfully." They loaded up the harmonium on the old cart and returned to Los Torres. As it turned out, I had already earned a good reputation among the people.

[Inserted from a previous draft] A few days later, a woman called for me to visit a sick man. She told me the man was a Negro. "Now" I wondered, "a Negro in this place among all this Mexican population?" She pointed out that the man was one of her lodgers, was working on one of the ranches, and only came back on Sundays. "What a strange case," I thought and went immediately.

When I entered the room, the Negro was laying in a corner on a few thin blankets. He didn't even have a mattress. Death was written in his face; he could no longer speak. There was no furniture, no chairs, but in another corner was his saddle. Since I did not know his religion, I opened his blue shirt and found the sign that indicated that he was one of my flocks. I did what I could and the poor man passed away in my arms. Even though his skin was black, I do believe his soul was as white as the snow when he left this earth.

But here's the strange part of this story. I had barely returned to the parish, when the same woman who called me to visit the Negro, approached me to let me know that she was making preparations for the black man's funeral and asked what I could do in this matter. I told her I would provide a church funeral.

"But," the woman snapped, "the deceased doesn't own anything but the saddle and I am claiming it—he was behind in his rent. I can't pay for the funeral and I will not let go of the saddle!"

Now I got mad and was tempted to grab her by the neck and kick her out. Had it been a man, he would have been out in seconds. I got angry: "Did I ask you for money or the saddle?"

The woman was not alone in this place thinking that a priest should be given as little compensation as possible and assuming that priests come here only to make money.

"If I wanted to make money, I wouldn't be in New Mexico, among you," I said.

"Today, I will start and bring some order into this place. Tomorrow morning, there will be a church funeral and next Sunday I will tell the community what I think. You won't have to pay a penny and you can keep the saddle. You may ride anywhere you want, but I won't go with you." I told the woman all that in Spanish, because she didn't speak any English. I am sure she understood my Spanish.

The next morning I held the funeral. Not only did I want to prove to the people that priests on these missions are not out to make money, but that he, indeed, needed to make a living. There wasn't a relief list yet, but had [Franklin Delano] Roosevelt been President then already, I would have immediately registered for that list. Instead, I had to find other means to improve my situation. In my next Sunday sermon I told the congregation the following.

My dear congregation:

I need to bring up a few issues today. You didn't have a priest for over a year, but now you do (and one with hair on his teeth, I thought to myself), one who has a big heart for his community. But you'll need to have some compassion for him as well. A priest, too, must eat, just like everybody else. I am used to eating simple meals, beans and chili, if there's nothing else to be had, although I do prefer, however, potatoes, meat, and vegetables. [....] You know the rules if you want to have a priest. Let's make some uniform rules here: All funerals and weddings will be free. But let me explain: The following Sunday after a funeral or a wedding, I will announce publicly how much money the relatives gave to the priest for his service. So if the marriage candidates are generous, it will be a splendid event, otherwise a rather simple ceremony. It will be up to you. Amen.

This was the end of my sermon and I believe it was a good one. It worked and none of my children wanted to be seen as cheap.

I need to point out that the members of my congregation were very nice people, and the longer I stayed in Chaparito the more I liked my parish. The people in the far-away missions were especially dear to me. One could find there true humanity and Christian love despite all the poverty surrounding them. There, one could still find the pure soul in a human being along with deep-seated religion. There wasn't much worldly education, but the highest education in form of God's will was there. I've often experienced people in automobiles or airplanes, who are closer to heaven as it goes, who are put in their places by the pure and simple, yet faithful Spanish Americans. Today, twenty-five years later, the Spanish Americans are no longer as pure as then, due to the influence by modern culture. It is to the detriment of the Spanish American population in New Mexico.

After a few days I wanted to go to the missions. I knew this would be a long trip, and my newly hired sacristan Don Isidro who would keep an eye on everything, gave me the necessary directions. One day, then, we left and traveled 35 miles in the buggy. People lived very isolated on farms and often miles away from the church. We arrived in the evening at the mission and had just unleashed the horses after this 35-mile trip, when a man rode up and reported a sick man nearby—an additional 30 miles.

I asked my sacristan if he knew the way. Certainly, he'd know the way but hasn't been there in over a year. We harnessed the horses again, and off we went. But never in my life had I seen such a trail, if one could call it that. We arrived late at night, only to start our trip back to the mission at four the next morning. I promised those people a mass and thus could not disappoint them. When I arrived at the chapel, I was not at all sorry to have made this trip back in the cold, because the people who hadn't heard a mass in over a year were very happy to see a priest.

I just remember another sick call to the same place. It was on a Sunday afternoon around two o'clock when the call came and I was about sixty miles away; that is 120 miles back and forth. The call was urgent, so I got ready quickly. Naturally, Don Isidro came along and we drove forty miles to a mission where we changed horses. To save time we decided on two good riding horses and took a shortcut through the mountains. It was already dark, and we recognized that we moved at a slower speed than with the buggy. We often had to dismount and lead the horses. Dead tired, we arrived shortly before midnight at the place. To my great surprise the call was not at all urgent. The old woman had a headache and wanted to see a padre. Since I was not prepared to read mass the next morning, I only ate something, and at six o'clock in the morning we were on our way back to Chaparito. We arrived at about three o'clock in the afternoon—we had covered at least 120 miles in twenty-four hours by buggy and by horse.

This was not quite as bad a trip, though, as the one I made a few years ago in Santa Fe. One day I was on a mission and before returning home, announced to the people to let me know if there were any sick people that I should visit. Nobody stepped forward and so I returned to Santa Fe. I was barely outside the village limits when man rode up to me and struck up a conversation. When we arrived in Santa Fe he followed me all the way to the cathedral. This, I thought, was strange and I asked him if he had any business in the cathedral. Yes, he said, there was a sick call in the same village where I just read mass this morning. Naturally, I had to return to the village. Oh, holy simplemindedness!

In the beginning it was quite difficult for me to adjust to my new environment. I am used to a certain comfort and when I am at home, well, I acted like being home. As mentioned earlier, I had no money when I arrived in Chaparito and basically started from ground zero. Helpful circumstances, however, were that my housekeeper had sent for her furniture from Santa Fe. Among the furniture were nice pieces and I soon had a comfortable home. She even sent for two big barrels of preserved fruits and other delicious things. My housekeeper was also a trained teacher who had some money saved and owned a house in Santa Fe which she rented out. She converted to Catholicism and was so devoted, she was always ready to help the good cause. Since she didn't understand any Spanish, so it was initially very difficult for her in Chaparito where at the time nobody spoke English. In one or two years, however, she learned to speak Spanish. She had not much of a choice with me being so often away at the missions, but to learn the language to maintain a conversation. "Give credit were credit is due" I say about my housekeeper and therefore I am not shying away from attesting to this woman's ability.

The reason why I was able to spend so much time in the parish of Chaparito was due to my housekeeper's sacrifices. She was the church organist and assembled a good choir. In the second year at the mission we bought a portable harmonium weighing only about fifty pounds. The poor people near the missions, with the exception of those in Los Torres, did not know what it meant to listen to a musical mass. If a particular festivity was coming up, the little harmonium was loaded into the buggy and off we went to the mission. A mass celebrated with a harmonium was a treat for the people—but also a great sacrifice to my housekeeper who drove for miles and miles in this buggy, regardless of wind and weather. But she did it to honor her Lord. And to tell the truth she even unselfishly donated her savings of $1500 and another $1500 from the sale of her house in Santa Fe to the missions. To improve the children's religious education and to help me out maintaining and improving the missions, she also taught public school in Chaparito and in Los Torres.

When I had Sisters work in Chaparito, my housekeeper could no longer teach there anymore and moved to Los Torres. There she lived in a small sacristy, which was furnished with only a small cooking stove, a little table, a chair, and a miserable portable bed. The floor in the sacristy was mud. To continue teaching children religion, she accepted the teaching position in Los Torres, and even provided religious classes after school.

Fridays she returned to Chaparito, attended to my quarters and prepared my meals for the coming week, which I then warmed up myself. When any festivities came up at one of the mission, we left on a Friday to have the people enjoy a musical mass that she presented on her harmonium. And the money she earned as a teacher? That went into my pockets for the missions. To the dear Lord this is a priceless deed, but people don't always acknowledge this.

There was a lot of work to do in the parish of Chaparito. There used to be a priest, my predecessor's predecessor, who had his own system to attend to the missions. He did not hold a permanent residence but lived out of his wagon. It was a customized vehicle with a few amenities, covered with canvas just like the covered wagons, and that's where the priest lived. When making a trip to the missions, his journey took at least two to three months. The wagon carried enough provisions, was even furnished with a table, a comfortable chair and a bunk bed for two, because his servant and sacristan always traveled with him. He took it easy on the horses, never rushed them, and wherever the night fell—whether in the mountains or in the plains—he set up camp. When he arrived at a mission, he got as comfortable as possible in a parishioner's house, stayed there for a few days and tended to the folks' religious needs.

Then he continued his journey to the next mission and again stopped for the night whenever dusk came regardless of how close to or far from his destination he was. This priest's sacristan himself once told me that one night after a three-month tour they arrived near Chaparito when darkness fell in. The sacristan who had his family in Chaparito would have liked to continue the last mile to Chaparito. Instead, the priest decided to call it a day and the horses were unhitched. The next morning, however, the horses were missing and the sacristan walked into the village to look for them finding them at home in their stable. The good padre waited patiently for the return of the horses. Slowly, then, they made the last mile into town where they rested for a few days only to start another long journey. This, now, was the ideal concept and people out in the missions knew that when the priest came he would stay with them for a few days.

My immediate predecessor was of a different kind. He worked as a missionary usually does, one day at one mission and another day at another mission until all missions were looked after. This priest, Father Plantard, was working hard and left many monuments of his work in Chaparito. Unfortunately, he gave up the mission too early. One night after a trip to Las Vegas, along with his housekeeper he was on his way back to Chaparito, when the horses stalled in the dark and the buggy with all its passengers were about to fall into a deep abyss. The housekeeper was able to jump out of the buggy and the horses broke out of their harness. Only the priest was stuck in the buggy and fell down the abyss. Since then Father Plantard was not the same anymore and I had to take over his duties.

Since the mission was left without a priest for about a year, it was a difficult new beginning. The chapels, in particular, were in poor condition and in some villages it was necessary to build new ones. During my time in Chaparito the following chapels were built or repaired: a new chapel made from stone was built in La Garita, in Conchas de Abajo, and in Sabinoso and the construction of the chapel in San Ramon was continued and finished. Throughout the missions, sacristies were built, and new roofs were put on some of the chapels like in Los Torres, Cañon Largo, and Variadera. In short, all chapels were restored or renovated.

Of all the challenging tasks among the many chapels and churches, the most demanding one was the improvement of the church in Chaparito. To renovate the church, a fence was set up, a fresh roof put on, and new windows inserted. The walls of the church were about three feet thick which made the work very dangerous. The interior of the church, too, had to be restored. Worth mentioning are the paintings of the monstrance and the two angels in front of the sanctuary. There was no confessional then, and the one I installed is still used today. All the statues, except the statue of the Holy Isidor, the patron saint of this church, arrived during my tenure.

Congregation of Maria children were organized in easy-to-reach places, and it was a pleasure to see all the children from Chaparito and other missions, dressed in white, participating in church festivities on Sundays. Every mission's congregation had one annual special day. Particular the congregations in Chaparito and in La Liendre flourished under the direction of Fidelia Tapia and Antonia Tapia.

It was my greatest pleasure to visit the missions and to travel for days from one place to another. I had to take care of fifteen chapels and it was quite often a sacrifice to visit all of them regularly within a month. It meant spending every night in a different bed, usually with very good but poor people who revered the priest. Some families' quarters—I don't want to mention their names—were so poorly furnished that I often spent a night on the floor or on a thin mattress.

For instance, once during a time of fasting I spent three days in Variadero. The people who lived nearby the little church were very nice but extremely poor; plus, they had a lot of children. The matriarch was over a hundred years old. Three of us went and to make this visit as nice as possible we also took along my housekeeper's portable harmonium. The weather was beautiful and so I had high expectations of this Easter trip. The chapel's sacristy in Variadero was small but that's where we had to spend three nights. I slept on a portable bed while the sacristan and my housekeeper and organist slept on mattresses spread out on the adobe floor. Over night, the weather turned bad and we experienced a real blizzard.

The people living in the vicinity could not attend mass and we could not leave the sacristy for two days. We were stuck in—and no other word fits—this hole, even when it was the sacristy. On the second day, we ran out of food. We could only brew black coffee on the stove. The horses in the stable had no food. My sacristan went out to find some food for the horses but no hay was available. Instead, he returned with 25 pounds of corn. On the third day the storm moved away, and in desperation we left for another mission in hope that we could find something to eat there, especially for the horses. The sacristan and the housekeeper rode in the buggy and for the next ten miles, I walked ahead of the horses looking for the right trail and to avoid dangerous deep ditches, which are so numerous out here in the plains.

This happened in March and the snow began to melt quickly. When we arrived at the next mission we found something to eat for ourselves, but there was still nothing for the horses, no hay at all. The following morning we left early to return to Chaparito about forty miles away. We walked very slowly because the horses were so weak. We arrived in the evening dead-tired, but to save the horses—too much corn at once seemed to be fatal—I had to stay up almost all night and play horse vet. I held five horses in Chaparito, one riding horse and four buggy horses. Since I was almost always on a journey to one of the missions, I had to use another pair of horses for the next trip.

I remember one of the missions with great pleasure. It is San Ramon, about fifty miles from Chaparito. There lived the good family of Jose Quintana and his good and pious wife Firminia. During one of my big trips, my sacristan and I arrived in San Ramon only to stop briefly because we wanted to visit the more distant missions first and stay in San Ramon on our way back.

When we came close to the next mission, we realized that we could not cross the river called "Rio Colorado" [possibly Rito Colorado, a creek northwest of Las Vegas] because of high waters. The old church was on this side of the river and only three very poor families lived here. We moved into the old sacristy, which was about to crumble at any moment. Naturally there was no bed, only two rickety old chairs. In addition, it started to rain and so I sent my sacristan, the faithful Isidro, to the next house to ask for something to eat and for two mattresses and a few blankets for the night.

It was summer, the corn was ripe and the first corn always tasted the best. Besides, green chili, the Spanish pepper, was ready and tasted spicy. Food was soon served and we would have liked a cup of coffee and a slice of bread, but our good but poor host had none of these luxury items in the house. Since there was nothing else to do after this meager meal we went to bed for a long night. The next morning, only the three families attended mass because those on the other side of the river could not cross. Still hoping the water might recede, we stayed another day. This may have been the longest day I have ever experienced. There was nothing to do but to pray, and one cannot do that all the time. Besides, the corn and the green chili caused my stomach to get upset rather than to cooperate a bit. Thereafter I hadn't even looked at green chili for about three months.

The next day the rain stopped and we hitched the horses early in the morning and were on our way back to San Ramon. My hope was to fulfill my duties better there. We arrived in San Ramon at noon and to our surprise it had not rained there at all. But it started to rain cats and dogs that evening. The good Don Jose and Dona Firminia had a small room prepared for us, which was really comfortably and always made me feel at home.

The house was not even built of adobe. Only posts were rammed into the ground, coated with mud, covered with a roof, and that was it. The Mexicans call this type of house Jacal. It was so comfortable and the family's spirit so touching that one could not help but feel at home. The house was so clean that I really felt good to be with these people, not even the rain bothered me. During the night, though, the roof started to leak and all night we moved the mattresses from one corner to another. In the morning only one dry spot was left. When I stepped into the living room, I was caught by surprise and had to laugh: the entire room was under water and to avoid further water damage, a big canvass was spread out like a tent. We spent the whole day and another night under this canvass. On the third day the rain stopped. The horses were immediately harnessed and we drove home fifty miles through mud and dirt. It was long after midnight when we arrived in Chaparito.

At that time there were about six hundred families living in the Chaparito parish, including all the missions. The missions were poor, but the people were ready to make every sacrifice and thus the priest was making a good, actually a very good living if one did not care for modern amenities. The one thing I should have done was to put some money aside for emergencies. I never thought of it and that was my fault. Every cent was put into the parish. Even my housekeeper and organist, who labored unselfishly, put her earnings and savings back into the parish and thus gained the affection of the people.

The successor to Archbishop Pitaval, New Mexico's greatest and most humble archbishop, [Thomas Daeger1919–1932] pointed out to me on several occasions the need to have some savings in case of an emergency. He also warned me not to use other people's money for mission purposes.

"I know what you have done for the missions," he said once, "but I will not live for ever." I never bothered to listen, because the archbishop himself did not follow his own advice in that respect. His work, too, was to save souls and his wallet was always empty. I was surprised over and over again of what kind of a missionary this man was. It is difficult to imagine his simplicity and love for his priests and to describe his benevolence.

Here I would like to mention a situation which I often remembered in my life. It was on his last visit to the parish of Chaparito. The entire trip took ten days, and in almost every one of the fifteen missions he held confirmations. One Saturday we arrived in San Ramon where we spent the night in the house of Don Jose y Dona Firminia. After the archbishop read the mass in the small chapel on Sunday, we continued to Conchas Abajo, another mission. There were four of us in a small two-seater carriage. The trip was some twelve miles long but the last two miles we walked while the sacristan, who substituted for my regular sacristan for a few days, and the mass servant rode with the horses and carriage over the rough trail. When we arrived, everybody was already waiting. I read mass and thereafter gave Confirmation.

The Archbishop enjoyed Las Conchas [Conchas Abajo], particularly since our hosts, the family Tenorio, prepared everything well for our stay. The old father Tenorio with his three daughters even asked the village people to stay for lunch, and subsequently we all ate an excellent meal under clear skies. Our archbishop, not surprisingly, was the honored guest at the table, and to his right side sat the old father Tenorio and to his left side his three daughters. This image is one of my fondest memories from my years as a missionary. But the day wasn't over yet.

We enjoyed ourselves so much that we almost forgot about the rest of our trip. Eventually, around four o'clock in the afternoon, we said good-bye and left for La Manga, where we were expected to give confirmation that evening. With the best wishes from all the people who continued to celebrate, we left. When we passed Los Conchas's small chapel, the archbishop commented about its beauty. A place that never before had had a church, I felt that I had accomplished something in my life.

It was twelve miles to La Manga, but I had reliable horses—a beautiful black and very sentimental one, which never needed a whip, just one word and the horse listened, and a smaller horse, but quite vital and obedient. About two miles into the trip, I brought the archbishop's attention to a so-called arroyo, which usually did not carry much water and was not dangerous to cross. This time, however, I could see the water already from a distance and was concerned. It was difficult to cross the arroyo when a lot of water was in it. There was a lot of water running in the arroyo, and since it was colored clay-red, it must have rained quite a bit elsewhere. I had the horses stopped and walked to the bank of the arroyo to check if it was possible to cross. I picked up a large stone and threw it into the strong current. It was too deep to cross at this spot, and if we were to miss the precise ford we might drown. When I returned to the buggy I explained that it was too dangerous to cross the ford, but the archbishop decided to risk a crossing in order not to disappoint the waiting people of La Manga. Otherwise we would have been forced to make a 25-mile detour.

Had I guided the horses myself, nothing might have happened, because I knew the passage. But instead, I instructed the sacristan how to drive the buggy and not to rush the horses.

"Let the horses find their way, they will get us to the other side," were my instructions. Thus, we drove slowly into the arroyo. The water immediately reached to the horses' chests, and we behind them in the buggy. The water quickly reached the box of the buggy.

"Slowly, slowly," I told the teamster, "let the horses find the way."

I believe when we reached the middle of the arroyo, the guy suddenly showed nerves. He pulled the rein in a manner that, not surprisingly, the horses moved to the right. The buggy bumped over a big rock, one of the wheels got caught between two rocks in the arroyo, and the buggy was stuck. I grabbed the rein while talking soothingly to the animals to stand quietly and there we were—trapped. I told the teamster: "Go into the water and stand in front of the animals, so that they don't move, or else the buggy may capsize." Turning to the archbishop, who had a surprised look on his face, I told him to stay in the buggy.

The coachman's name was Frank and the mass servant's was Juan. I held the rein and Frank stepped into the water, which immediately reached to his chest. While he held the horses, I stepped off the buggy, unhitched the horses and led them to the other side of the arroyo. I then returned to the buggy and tried to free the wheel.

The archbishop sitting in the carriage watched from above until he realized that the three of us could not move the buggy. So, he took his shoes off, then his socks, his jacket, vest, archbispal collar, and finally his shirt putting them along with his ring onto the seat of the buggy and only wearing his underwear, jumped into the water. He pulled the lance, while we worked the wheel, but we just could not move it out from under the rocks.

In the excitement we forgot to remove from underneath the seats our spare cloths and the archbishop's suitcase filled with his cassock, mitre, and even a beautifully stitched choir shirt or surplice, a gift he received on the day of his consecration. Now everything was soaked with the muddy water. I fetched his clothes from the seat and carried them along with the rest of our stuff ashore. The archbishop excused himself for a few minutes and returned moments later wearing dry clothes from his retreat. But the three of us stayed wet because we had no dry cloths to change into. Everything in our suitcases was wet and unusable from the mud. We gave up retrieving the buggy. Leaving the archbishop behind at the arroyo, we walked to the nearest house, a mile away.

Unfortunately the owners were still at the confirmation celebration and the house was locked. Since I knew the family well, I decided to break into the house and unlocked the only door to the outside. In the house I found myself a pair of trousers, which were ripped at the knees, and an old jacket. I don't want to mention what the others found to wear, but a blanket protected everybody. When we returned to where the archbishop was waiting, my buggy was on this side of the water.

During our absence people came by who pulled the buggy out of the moving current. We hitched the horses again and, dressed as we were, rode to the next mission. Since it was getting late already, the people of La Manga sent out a search party to look for us. This cavalcade was obviously quite surprised to see us in our outfits. Only the archbishop looked dignified. After we arrived in La Manga, the archbishop went immediately to the church while our hosts found us some better clothes and gave us the opportunity to warm up. When I arrived at the chapel, I saw the archbishop in his wet robe holding mass for the people before confirmation. After the confirmation we had dinner and then everything we needed to have cleaned was being washed. Cassocks and other things were hanged on the clothesline to dry. The following morning, however, the archbishop's beautiful surplice had disappeared [Küppers gives no indication of what might have happened to it]. There was one family in La Manga that owned an automobile with which they took us to another mission, while the sacristan return with my horses and buggy back to Chaparito. In the afternoon we arrived by car in Chaparito.

On the following day, 10 August, the people of Los Torres celebrated the day of the Holy Laurentius. Years ago the villagers discovered in the Twin Mountains a chapel carved into a boulder. It took a good hour to reach the top of the mountain. In order to reinforce the people in this pious exercise, I have held mass in this chapel every year on 10 August. Almost everybody from the region participated in this event. Some years earlier I erected a big cross on one of the peaks, and the procession moved after mass from the chapel to the cross, where I then held my sermon. Near the chapel was a small spring where we enjoyed a snack after the festivities.

It was 9 August 1920, and it was the last confirmation that I administered as priest of Chaparito. My tenure in Chaparito under the administration of the archbishop [Daeger] came to an end. On the morning of the 10th I planned on holding mass high up in the Twin Mountains. But there was a big surprise for me. The archbishop informed me the evening before: "You may say mass in the morning in church and I will read mass in the little chapel in the mountains." All my protests were in vain. In the morning I drove the archbishop personally in the buggy to Los Torres where the hike on foot began.

This is a situation in which one recognizes the spirit of Archbishop Daeger. The people were surprised that an archbishop would give them such honor. He celebrated Holy Mass and then all of us ascended in procession to the cross, where he gave a speech worthy of a spiritual leader. Never before were the people as thankful as they were on this day. After a simple and frugal meal we descended and returned from Los Torres back to Chaparito. From there the archbishop returned to Santa Fe.

A plaque reminds people that the beloved Archbishop Daeger read mass on 10 August 1920 in the small chapel in the mountain, the highest point in the parish of Chaparito. It was also the last time ever that I was on this mountain, because soon thereafter I was transferred. No mass has been read since that time in the chapel of

St. Lawrence in the Twin Mountains or, as they are called in Spanish, Los Gemelos.

***

It was always my main concern to work for the Church. This is the duty of every priest. What I have to say now is not meant to hurt the pious feelings of my readers but only to show how devoted I was to my work. Some might even call it fanaticism.

In the parish of Chaparito was a place called Trementina. It was a small village nicely situated, about thirty-five miles from Chaparito. The little village was on a slight elevation and had a Presbyterian school and church, even a small hospital. The school and church rose above the wide-open plains which stretched for miles in every direction. The village was surrounded by three of my missions: San Raphael, San Ramon, and Las Conchas. During the winter months, most children from this Catholic mission attended the Presbyterian school in Trementina. Obviously, I did not like that at all, and since the church watches over the children in matters of belief, I prohibited the parents to send their children to the Protestant school.

In those days the public school system was rotten in these remote districts and none of my three missions could exhibit a schoolhouse. For a few months each year school was held in a private home at one of the missions. The Presbyterian school, on the other side, was open nine months out of the year. In the event of sickness the locals also enjoyed the hospital services instead of traveling a hundred miles to see the nearest doctor.

I was not very successful in my efforts to keep the children away from the school. Fortunately, I knew a few good Catholic politicians in my three mission districts and I developed a plan. One Sunday, three of my best politician friends came to see me in Peñasco [it should read "Chaparito"] where I already cued another friend in on my plan. From there we drove to Las Vegas, incidentally in the same car which brought me to Chaparito in a snowstorm years ago, and informed the most powerful and most influential politician of San Miguel County, Secundino Romero, of our plan.

The plan was to draw a few new school districts and to keep Trementina in a distant corner of one of them. Secundino Romero and the other influential politicians decided instantly to form new districts and to redraw the borders according to my specifications. A few days later I heard that a licensed surveyor had already measured the three districts. Now it was possible to install school principals for the new districts who made sure that good teachers were hired for each. This move hurt Trementina and it was the beginning of the end for this town.

Then I started to build the new chapel in Las Conchas and slowly formed a sense of community, away from the Presbyterian influence in Trementina. Obviously, this did not endear me to the Presbyterian pastor, but we became good friends eventually when he was called to Embudo, where I was by then the parish priest.

It was the principle of my ecclesiastical work to give our Spanish American children, who were often simply called Mexican, what all children needed most: a good education. For that purpose I wanted to employ Sisters. Now that was difficult to achieve, because Chaparito was a small hamlet without any amenities. Even drinking water had to be brought up from the river, and to climb down to the river was by itself a sacrifice. If that wasn't enough, the river water was undrinkable unless it was put away over night so that the dirt would sink and the clearness would become visible. I know about the demands Sisters have, and I don't blame them, as an order or individually, to be concerned about their health and to act accordingly.

The house in Chaparito was an L-shaped one-story building, which was easily converted into a Sister dormitory. Naturally, I though that the Sisters should also take over the small public school. For the parish children, I intended to build a small parish school and considered accepting boarding children for a small compensation. The thought of giving the children everything I possibly could, kept me moving. One should keep in mind that Chaparito was not a rich parish, but a priest who wanted to save his money could have certainly done so. This, however, never crossed my mind.

In those years a priest's spiritual exercises were held privately. The archbishop appointed three priests who had to do them in a monastery. This rule was later changed because the priests, particularly when they were friends, had a grand time together. One day, I was order to see the Jesuits in Las Vegas to do my own exercises. After the three days of exercises were over, I received news that a young man from Philadelphia arrived and was waiting for me [1915].

Four years or so ago, I met the family in Philadelphia. The old grandmother, who was still living then, always maintained that there was a family relationship between her family and mine in Germany. I never cared much for that, but I was happy that "our Harry" as he was known in his family, was visiting me in New Mexico. Not surprisingly, we began to talk of family matters. After finishing his law education in Philadelphia, Harry wanted to try his luck out West, which he eventually did as he is now a well-known lawyer in San Francisco. His visit to New Mexico was the best thing that could have happened to me: I had a friend and companion and we got along splendidly.

Harry was the one who helped me to make my school plans a reality. After I taught him horseback riding, we rode often together to the missions, and since he also happened to be an excellent singer, he soon became irreplaceable. It was particularly beautiful when he sang in the choir in Chaparito. Once I had completed my drawings for the school building, we began our work. Every morning after breakfast we left for the nearby quarry where we broke rocks. We even used some dynamite to break them. Day in and day out for weeks, we labored in the quarry to produce stones. Once in a while a child from my parish came to help us. I simply had no money to pay the people.

In Chaparito, already, I had a reputation of being rich because I did what I wanted to do and built what was necessary. The money I earned in the parish just remained in the parish, and in addition, my housekeeper helped with her earnings as teacher. Since the people wanted to be paid, Harry and I did all the work ourselves. It looks like easy work here in these pages, but in reality it was hard and dangerous labor and neither one of us had any experience with dynamite: I, a priest, and Harry, an academician. Eventually I had to pay the people to transport the stones to the site to build the school. Slowly but surely the building took shape. We did the entire woodwork such as floor and roof, etc. alone. The parish house was eventually converted into a dormitory for the Sisters and an old house was purchased and comfortably decorated.

But the question still remained how to attract Sisters? As far as I remember I wrote to many Sister congregations, but to no avail. One day I received an unexpected telegram from [the Republic of] Cuba, in which the Sisters offered to take over the school in Chaparito. It was sent by the Sisters of the Immaculate Heart of Maria, who belonged to the Spanish province and had worked for years in Mexico. They had a branch in Mazatlan, Mexico, from where they were expelled. In the telegram, they asked for travel money. I wrote a letter back accepting their offer and mailed, if I remember correctly, $100.00. In my letter I noted that five Sisters were necessary and promised to reimburse them for the rest of their travel expenses. The Sisters' dormitory was ready yet I had no furniture and no money to buy any.

Spontaneously and with little preparation as usual—my biggest fault in life next to too much trust in friends—one early morning about four o'clock, I left Chaparito for Las Vegas. Determined to turn the future presbytery into a convent, I took my housekeeper along, as I did not know anything about the needs of Sisters. That day I bought a thousand dollars worth of furniture on credit. I don't remember how I ever paid that back, but I did. We returned the same day in our buggy to Chaparito, all in all 70 miles. It takes quite some enthusiasm to undertake these kinds of adventures.

The day the Sisters were supposed to arrive finally came. The house was ready and, as I thought, fully furnished, with a dorm for 12 interns. I agreed with the county or provincial school superintendent that two of the sisters were to teach in the small public school and two more in my own parochial school for the mission children. Then the day of arrival was here. One of my neighbors in Chaparito had recently purchased an automobile, which he let me borrow. I drove, or rather was chauffeured, to Las Vegas since I did not know how to drive a car. In Las Vegas I chartered a second bigger car to bring the Sisters back to Chaparito.

I was waiting at the station full of expectation and anticipation when the train arrived at half past one in the afternoon. Initially one Sister, then another one, stepped off the train, and I was right there to welcome them. But then more Sisters got off the train until there were ten Sisters and a Mexican girl in front of me. My heart almost sank: there were a total of eleven women, when I needed only five of them.

I was first introduced to the Provincial who spoke an excellent Spanish. Since I responded in English, the Mother Superior stepped in to help out, but her English was as rough as my Mexican Spanish. Only one of the Sisters spoke English very well, all other communicated in Spanish only. Asking them to remain on the station for a moment to wait for the cars, I excused myself in a hurry. I ran to the next telephone and ordered a third automobile to accommodate all the women.

My only thought was what to do with so many Sisters in poor Chaparito. Finally everybody was distributed among the three cars and I explained to the Sisters that we still had a drive of thirty miles to Chaparito ahead of us. I reminded the Sisters that Chaparito was only a small place, but the Provincial responded to this, that she was under the impression that Chaparito must be quite sizable as there are, according to my own letter, fourteen missions. How will all this end, I thought, but as the saying goes "I made my bed and now have to lie in it." In the meantime it started to rain and the cars had to crisscross very slowly over the slippery road. After the three-hour drive we arrived in Chaparito in pouring rain.

The people had waited patiently in front of the church, though some fled the rain and sought cover in the church. I had told the organist that upon my return I would initiate the Te Deum, but I had already lost all enthusiasm. I only gave praise and did not even welcome the good Sisters. I accompanied the Sisters to their house and pointed to their new living quarters explaining that I had only prepared for five Sisters. The Provincial Superior replied that her rule was that any branch had to consist at least of nine Sisters and that she would find work for all of them. "Now you have at least a home," I said, "and no Pancho Villa or Venustiano Carranza will force you to leave." Then I took my leave and return to my own poor house, contemplating and thinking about the things to come. All in all it went better than I thought because nuns usually find a way to make it work.

I previously had the opportunity to work with Mexican nuns. One day, two nuns from Parral, Mexico, came to Chaparito and asked to be taken in. They brought along a Mexican girl who must have been of a noble race because her facial features were beautiful and pure. I almost agreed to take them in, but since the nuns did not speak English, I had to think it over. The next morning I saw the Mexican girl with long open hair enter the grocery store and shortly thereafter she was smoking a cigarette in front of my house. I became careful and found an excuse about the delay of a branch in Chaparito.

I promised to do everything in my power to help the Sisters, particularly after they told me about the terrible persecutions against religious persons in Mexico and described the incredible sufferings and pain nuns had to endure there. I did everything I possibly could for the nuns, but now and then I was disappointed. First, only one Sister, born in Mexico to a Mexican mother and an Irish father, could speak English. The Provincial Superior, who soon left again, spoke only Spanish, and the local Mother Superior spoke only broken English. How could I send Sisters who did not speak English, to the public school? And the one who spoke English I wanted to keep for my parochial school. Thus, I sent the Mother Superior, who knew broken English into one classroom, and another Sister who did not know English—well—into the other classroom. When the school superintendent [Dr. DeMarais whom he identified as a good friend in another draft] visited to inspect the school, the only English-speaking Sister guided him through the classrooms trying to cover up the situation as best as possible. This was not a sin, but it just wasn't right, and eventually the situation turned out to be fatal.

I made one big mistake. Although I had the permission of Archbishop Pitaval to find Sisters for Chaparito, I unintentionally neglected to tell him that I actually accepted Sisters. He was not happy about the Sisters, probably, because they needed to speak English. But the fact remained, the Sisters were here, and I felt responsible for them, and was fond of them because they were good.

After two months with the Sisters in Chaparito, confirmation in the missions came up. It was during Archbishop Pitaval's tenure. Naturally, I accompanied him to the missions, and we were to return to Chaparito on a Saturday. During our trip the archbishop never mentioned the Sisters even though I tried several times to steer the conversation toward them—but to no avail.

I recommended that the people of Chaparito await the archbishop in a festive procession outside of town. When we arrived back in Chaparito on time, all the villagers were waiting for us at the village limits, first the children with the Sisters and then the adults. One of the children welcomed the archbishop on behalf of the village people. The archbishop was delighted and talked with the children, but not with the Sisters. These poor women, expelled from Mexico, must have felt it. In the church the archbishop said only a few words and we retreated to the parish house. I took an opportunity to sneak into the Sisters' dorm to comfort them. After dinner in the parish house, the archbishop still had not mentioned the Sisters. I was in a very bad mood since I was in support of the Sisters. I would like to mention here, that I am not criticizing but just telling the facts.

Unfortunately, in the morning something happened, which was fatal for the Sisters' stay. The archbishop held the early service. The little church was packed and nearly all the people received communion. When the archbishop took the goblet, he immediately slammed it back onto the altar. I immediately walked over to him and he asked me in a low but angry voice:

"Who filled the carafe?"

"The Sisters did it as always," I responded.

"Smell what's in there," he ordered. I sniffed and the bouquet smelled like whiskey. The poor Sisters unintentionally erred with catastrophic consequences. After the service, the archbishop requested to see the sacristan.[1] The archbishop told her in no uncertain terms what had happened. Listening to the archbishop's harsh words, she started to cry, and I told the archbishop: "You will not say another word to the Sister, go back to the house, and finish your breakfast." I returned to the sacristy and prepared everything for the second mass, which I was to hold. When I returned to the house, the archbishop said to me:

What am I supposed to tell the people after mass? The Sisters are not my responsibility, and especially since they teach in the public school, I cannot get involved in this matter. I tell you now as I intended all along: You made a big mistake to have the Sisters come here to Chaparito without my permission. I will tell the people that and also that I, as the Archbishop, have nothing to do with them.

I looked at the archbishop and only stuttered "What?" This was all I could get out.

So he continued: "This is how it will be, you can do with the Sisters what you want and I will not have any responsibilities."

Turning red, I jumped up and screamed: "This is the thanks for all my labor and efforts? You gave me permission to look for Sisters, you did not bring up any conditions for the search, and besides, they were the only ones willing to come to this godless place; and they are treated like this?"

I had tears in my eyes but continued: "If you risk talking to the people like that, and in the process humiliate the poor Sisters, then I know what I will do in front of you and all the people out there, regardless of the consequences. Now you do what you want; you are the archbishop." I left the room and went to the sacristy where I cried bitterly. I made my decision.

The High Mass was Coram Episcopo [Episcopal Court] in front of the bishop. It is difficult to describe how I felt. I know I am a very emotional man who takes everything to heart instead of dancing to the music. After mass I went to the sacristy, took off my ornaments, and returned immediately to the church.

The archbishop had already begun to talk when I sat down in one of the chairs in the sanctum. I looked at him, and my surprise was endless that I didn't move. The archbishop talked respectfully about the Sisters and the wonderful work they did with the children. Even I received a small, but unnecessary praise. I wasn't sure what to think of this all. He spoke for about an hour and seemed sincere in what he said. The Sisters were very happy after so much misery. Then it was confirmation and everything went well. After all was over I asked the archbishop for permission to say a few words. I thanked him and announced that the public examination in catechism would be at three o'clock. Thereafter there would be special greeting for the archbishop in the parish school and a short program. The Sisters were prepared. In the sacristy the archbishop asked me how I felt. I knelt and kissed his ring.

In the afternoon was examination. All the children and adults were present. Religious studies were my field and the children were excellently prepared, even when the archbishop himself started to ask questions. Then it was time for the little program the children prepared in the parish school. The program contained a number by my housekeeper who was also the teacher at Chaparito until the Sisters arrived, with a folk dance by the smallest schoolgirls. The archbishop thanked everybody but especially pointed to my housekeeper, whom he had known since the days in Santa Fe, as one of the best teachers. This statement must have hurt the Sisters, and I knew now for certain, that the Sisters could not stay in Chaparito.

As work with the children was my favorite task, I tried always to improve their lot, and usually discussed everything with the Sisters. I did have some enemies in Chaparito, though, (whom I will discuss in the end of this), and feared that I might lose in the matter of public education. I was not afraid when my children were at stake and was prepared to go through thick and thin for them. I wanted to obtain better public school buildings and contacted the school board, and encouraged all voters—men and women[2]— to cast their vote in that respect.

Election Day came. I did a lot of work preparing for this election, but so did my enemies. As far as I could tell the votes "for" and "against" would be very close. My opponents used the argument that taxes would rise sharply if the new school building were approved. Capital outlay along with the interest would be very high, and therefore the taxes would increase.

A few days prior to the election I talked to the Sisters: "In case we run the danger of losing the election, you have to vote, at least those of you who are eligible to vote." They promised to do so, and the day of election came. I did not do much that day but received regular word of how things stood. Toward four o'clock I received news that a family, who promised to vote for the school bond, had not done so yet. So I got up and walked them myself to the voting booth. Afterwards I learned they had voted against me. Half an hour prior to closing the election, word came to me that the Sisters had to save the election. I went to tell the Sisters to be ready to go with me to the voting office about fifteen minutes before closing.

A new school building would have been in their interest, but what happened? The Mother Superior explained to me that the Sisters were not allowed to vote without the expressed permission of the Provincial. I blew up when I heard that, and blamed the Sisters for promising me their vote in case of an emergency. In all this uproar I forgot to cast my own vote, and my opponents won, as far as I remember, by one vote [in an earlier draft, there was a four vote difference]. I never forgot this defeat.

But I was fine with the Sisters, and they did very good work. When I returned from the missions I usually stopped by the Sisters' dormitory and handed the money I made in the missions over to them. One day I received $80.00 from the missions and after I returned home, I went to see the Sisters turned my pockets inside out and dropped the money onto the table.

The same Congregation, to which the Sisters belonged, had another branch in San Miguel, Mexico. Those sisters, too, had to flee under the regimes of Villa and Carranza and escaped to the United States. Since they had difficulties finding a permanent home, word arrived in Chaparito that they would like to stay temporarily here. The Mother Superior asked my permission to keep them here for now. I never thought to deny this request, but was concerned: "How can we feed them? This means nine more Sisters. But just let them come, our Lord will take care of them." So, shortly thereafter nine more Sisters arrived, which raised the total to eighteen.

Soon, food was in short supply. The Sisters' house was big and roomy to accommodate them, but food was the problem. I went out to the missions, and told the people about the persecuted Sisters, and collected for their cause. To a few nearby missions, I even took along some Sisters, as for example to Los Torres, a small and poor hamlet of fifteen families. The collection in the chapel, as far as I can remember, came to eighteen dollars, which was perhaps all they had. Obviously the Sisters could not remain in Chaparito but had to find another permanent place.

Since the Sisters maintained the public school, they had to be qualified according to the laws of New Mexico. This meant that the Sisters had to attend an annual summer institute in which they were trained to be teachers. This summer something happened, but I am not quite sure what occurred and how. It is easy to understand that the [Mexican] Sisters who knew little English would not pass their exams. But language should not be the determining factor, because teaching is beyond the English language—it is a didactical issue. They were excellent teachers with no match, and it would have been easy for me to come to an arrangement with the New Mexican school board, because the board was always eager to hire good teachers. The Sisters could already teach English in school, just like today certain high school teachers, including Sisters, do not speak the Spanish language but still teach it.

Like I said I am not certain what exactly happened, but one day two Sisters came back from Santa Fe and immediately upon their return came to see me. Usually no Sister came to visit me in the parish house; instead, I came to see them in their quarters. They told me that Archbishop Pitaval did not accept their visit, and did not even offer them a chair when they called on him. When, shortly after the complaint, I visited Santa Fe, I laid blame on the Archbishop for the discourtesy toward my Sisters. His response was that he treated them well and with respect, which gave me reasons for concern. In addition, my attention was directed toward a newspaper clip, which more or less suggested that in a certain town a priest allowed Sisters, who were not sufficient in the English language, to teach public school. The whole story seemed somewhat far-fetched but it could not continue like this much longer. I blamed the Archbishop Pitaval and wrote him a letter accordingly on 16 May 1917:

> [Original English] Most Rev. Archbishop:
> The check for the Parochial School was received yesterday. I will thank the Extension for same. At the same time I will notify Rev. E.B. Ledvina that the parochial school at Chaparito was discontinued on account of the uncalled for, unfriendly attitude of Your Grace against my poor refugee Sisters.

I had no right [to accuse the Archbishop] because I think all had some fault at this situation. Perhaps I had to accept most of the blame, because I should not have hired Spanish and Mexican Sisters. First of all, they only came reluctantly not having been able to find another home, and secondly, I wanted them to teach in the public education system thus receiving their monthly school pay. Those who want to live in America and want to receive state or federal salaries, have to learn to speak and live like Americans.

Then, the Sisters had to accept their share of blame. They knew that English was necessary but came anyway to the United States. They should have known that they wouldn't be happy during their initial years until they adjusted to American conditions and culture. On 13 May 1917, I informed the Sisters in writing of the reasons why they could not remain in Chaparito. One of the reasons was that the branch in Chaparito was meant to be only temporary, as the Sisters themselves told me. Archbishop Pitaval knew exactly why he did not approve this branch, but he could have told me. Then we could have quietly looked for other Sisters to replace the Spanish Sisters. That way Chaparito would have continued to have Sisters.

During longer stays in Chaparito I made it a habit, especially during the summer time, to go visit the Sisters for a relaxing chat after dinner. One evening I did just that and made conversation with the Sisters who had all gathered on the so-called placita. We discussed the sad conditions in Mexico and I voiced the wish that I would like to find soon a good, permanent home for the poor persecuted Sisters. The next morning when I walked over to the Sisters' chapel, my surprise was great when only some of the original Sisters were there. I did not know what to think of it and when I asked, the response was "The Sisters left early this morning to found a new branch elsewhere." [The Jesuits in El Paso, Texas, offered them a new home.]

"But how," I asked.

"We ordered two automobiles from Las Vegas which took them to the train station." I was speechless. After all I had done for them! There was not one word of thanks; truthfully, all they did was to disappear secretly. Experiences like these obviously made me timid, and then the Sisters look often surprised when the priest is not all too friendly in his demeanor.

It isn't difficult to imagine that I had a hard time ahead of me once the Sisters left. But the reasons had little to do with the Sisters' departure. Rather, difficulties always occur when a Catholic cannot find the time to receive the sacraments, but wants to receive all the privileges of the Church. Inevitably, the public outcry turns against the priest who denies the privileges. This is what happened when an agitation started against me in Chaparito. I was even publicly accused to have broken windows and doors in the sisters' quarters and other things. All I can say is that I haven't shunned any effort or labor, nor money and lived the life of a pauper. I gave my own parish house to the sisters to use, living happily in quarters not worthy of a priest—such a priest who sacrifices so much, should expect some scarifies from others as well. Eventually, and out of desperation, I sold the house and built a small four-room living house in Chaparito.

This is the trouble with these United States. The buildings we live in have to be comfortably equipped, while some poor father of a family toils endlessly and works his hands bloody only to give his children a simple education. My heart goes out to the poor Mexicans' living conditions, with their ragged clothes, while we sit always at a good table, even in New Mexico.

[Inserted from previous draft] A small stream ran through Chaparito which was used to water the nearby fields and as such it was a life line for the population. Then a land company began to build a dam far away from Chaparito. It wanted to use the water for the reservoir and then to irrigate land north of Chaparito. I protested against it and pointed out that there would not be any water left for the local population. But the dam was built, and today Chaparito as well as a few other places are deserted; many people moved away.

In addition, it was claimed that Chaparito and two other communities were situated in a land grant and that people in Chaparito had no right to let their cows, sheep, and goat graze on nearby land. I took the initiative, since I believe this to be a priest's task to look out for his people's material well-being. There were long negotiations with lawyers and politicians. The locals paid attention when I explained that it was better to find justice from the courts instead of leaving everything to those greedy for land. We prevailed in this case and everybody won the right to use a few thousand acres as grazing land. Unfortunately, the land company talked many people out of their rights for as little as twenty or fifty dollars and in turn, the company placed far too many of their own sheep, cattle, and goats on the land that there wasn't enough food for all of them. There was nothing else I could do because in the final analysis it was the people's right to sell their properties.

Finally, I had one additional problem during my time in Chaparito. I was born in Germany and, if I remember correctly, I began my paperwork for naturalization to become a United States citizen before the European War [World War I]. I was the only German in Chaparito and when the United States declared war on Germany I was still not a citizen. Obviously, I was sad to see this war against my homeland, but I knew my duties. America was my new home. [He had to buy Liberty Bonds and was called "El Aleman" or even "El Estrangero [sic]."—Peter Küppers became a U.S. citizen in December 1920] [end previous draft insert].

In all the years here in Chaparito, I had never the slightest difficulties in any of my missions—all fourteen of them. In September 1917 my housekeeper took over the public school in Los Torres and lived in the small sacristy. Initially, the people wanted to make available to her a small two-room house. Since that house was without roof and there was no money to fix it, I tried to repair it myself—poorly as it turned out—with used materials. When I was done, a big hailstorm went right through the roof and it rained into the house that we were forced to find shelter in the school building and to spend the night. It was then that we decided she should live in the sacristy and left it at that. I was almost always out in the missions and generally returned on Fridays to officiate the Sunday services in Chaparito.

In 1920, Archbishop Daeger arrived for the first time to confirmation exercises in Chaparito. From the beginning of his tenure he was favorably disposed toward me, and we became friends early on. On 13 April 1919 when the newly elected Bishop spent time in Cincinnati to prepare for his consecration, he wrote me a nice letter, which I still have. After the confirmation in Chaparito was over, and after he held mass on the Twin Mountains, which I mentioned earlier, he asked me: "How about I give you another parish?"

"But why?" I asked him immediately.

"You are here now for already seven years, you traveled a lot," he responded, "and as soon as I have an opening which requires less physical labor, I will give it to you."

I did not like that at all. All the people here were faithful and very nice. I asked him to give me at least another year to bring things into order. Then my successor would have a nice parish. I also asked him to look for Sisters, American Sisters to be sure, and he told me he would make sure to bring Ursuline Nuns to Chaparito.

The archbishop was barely a few days back in Santa Fe, when I received a letter from him, reminding me of his promise, and since a parish will open up very soon, he would give it to me. The priest of Peñasco had resigned and the archbishop gave him the Chaparito parish. I was to report to my new parish on 20 September [1920]. I immediately wrote back, that our agreement was that I could stay in this parish for another year. His answer came quickly and in no uncertain terms, I was ordered to be in Peñasco on the assigned date. So there was nothing to do but to obey. I not even knew where Peñasco was located, I only heard about it as a place where people had no spiritual foundation, and where people frequently were secretly shot and killed. So that was my nice new parish.

Initially, I did not mention anything to my parishioners but when the time to leave came closer, I had to announce it. I did not tell them when I was leaving Chaparito. I went to visit some of the missions to say good-bye and remember that tears were flowing freely. In Chaparito I prepared my departure, when I heard all of a sudden that a delegation of townspeople left without my knowledge to see the archbishop to ask him to let me stay in Chaparito. Naturally the request was denied. Then the people planned petitions in all the missions to be sent to the archbishop. When I heard about this petition drive, I forbade it and explained to the people that they were wasting their time and I had to admit I was leaving Chaparito knowing I accomplished a lot although I felt sorry for the missions.

I decided on a Sunday morning as the day for my departure, a day the people did not expect me to leave. The day before, I sent my two best horses and the buggy to Los Torres; from there they were to be taken to Peñasco. A neighbor, whose two daughters entered the clergy under my administration, was ready Sunday morning to take me to Las Vegas. I rang the bells at five o'clock in the morning and gave the first sign for mass. At six o'clock I gave the last sign. This was somewhat unusual and all the people gathered in the church. I did not hold a sermon, instead after silent mass, I turned to the people and told them that I was about to leave. I thanked everybody and returned to the sacristy. The people followed and left small presents with me, and I saw lots of tears in their eyes.

In my neighbor's house I took a cup of coffee, stepped up into the buggy and off we went to Peñasco. On our way out of town we had to stop often for well-wishers waiting along the street. When we passed the house of an old and poor woman, Dona Conception, she gave me all the money she owned. She stood in the door waiting for me, and asked me to step into her house, and as she was always a good soul, I accepted. She disappeared for a second into an adjacent room and upon her return put twenty dollars [in an earlier draft, she gave him fifty dollars] into my hand. I had to accept the money, her only money. This is love.

When we reached the proximity of Los Torres, the bells of the church and of the Penitentes' morada rang and all the villagers gathered to say good-bye. I had to step off the buggy, visit the church and say a few words. Then everybody knelt and asked for my blessing. This indicated love for a priest.

[Inserted from a previous draft] For those who would like to know what work was done during my seven year tenure, for those I write down the works; those who don't want to read it, can refrain from it, as everything is noted in heaven.

> Chaparito: Church completely renovated; new roof installed; big, new windows put in; new confessional acquired; nice and big statues of saints purchased for the church; new enclosure built around the church; new Christmas manger purchased.
>
> New school building constructed; a new presbytery built; the old big presbytery renovated and furnished for use as convent; fountain installed; sister chapel constructed.
>
> Mission of Los Torres: Church or chapel renovated; new roof installed; new church bell purchased.
>
> Mission of La Liendre: Church roof fixed; new enclosure constructed around the chapel; interior renovated and new Stations of the Cross acquired; harmonium purchased; two small side altars built; big statue of St. Anthony acquired; sacristy furnished to be inhabitable, with bed, wash desk, and desk and chairs.

Mission of Concepcion: new roof installed on chapel; two small side altars built.

Mission of San Augustin: new roof installed on big chapel; new Stations of the Cross acquired; a big statue of the Sacred Heart Jesus acquired for the main altar.

Mission of Aguilar: new sacristy built; furnished with bed and accessories; new Stations of the Cross purchased; the mission does not exist anymore.

Mission of Corazon: A nice little chapel was already in existence and I did not have to make many improvements; confessional acquired.

Mission of Trementina: sacristy built; new Stations of the Cross acquired.

Mission of San Ramon: completed unfinished chapel; new sacristy built; new Stations of the Cross and new statue purchased.

Mission of Sabinoso: beautiful new chapel built from stones and floor from the finest material; new Stations of the Cross purchased.

Mission of Cañon Largo: new roof installed on large chapel; sacristy furnished with bed and other necessary items.

Mission of Bariadero: new roof installed on chapel; new Stations of the Cross acquired; sacristy furnished to function as lodging.

Mission of Conchas Abajo [Las Conchas]: nice new chapel built from stones; small altar made from marble acquired; Stations of the Cross purchased.

Mission of La Manga: new sacristy built; new church bell purchased; also new Stations of the Cross acquired.

Mission of La Garrita: new, beautiful, spacious chapel built from stone, also with first rate flooring; two-room sacristy built, also with stones; furnished sacristy with necessary items; altar and Stations of the Cross.

It is easy to write down all these achievements, but to do them in seven years was no small task. My territory covered four thousand English square miles. Regarding the spiritual education, one of my successors gave me a compliment by noticing that the people were well educated and attended church and sacraments avidly. I liked organizing and I was particularly proud of my Children of Mary congregations which I established in almost every mission.

I don't think anyone could claim that I was lazy at work. Today there is no priest anymore in the parish as nobody expects a priest to live his life that way. But I did well then, although I could not afford an automobile to visit the far-away places; instead I had to visit the people by horse or buggy. And yet the people were not neglected, were visited on a regular basis, and received services regularly. I took my priestly duties seriously, was a good father to all, and still today remember my missions around Chaparito with fondness and gratitude. In Chaparito itself, however, I did make some sad experiences. Still, if I had my health back, I would love to return to this kind of hard work, but our dear lord put a stop to it, as I am health-wise a sick man.

"Thy will may be done in earth, as it is in heaven."
Amen.
[end insert]

Soldiers of the Cross

In his book *Soldiers of the Cross*, Archbishop J.B. Salpointe [1885–1894] estimated the number of priests who worked in New Mexico under the Mexican reign to be thirty-five. This period contained thirty-eight years of work by this small number of priests in a territory larger than 100,000 square miles. This was hard work, especially when one considers that the roads were bad (if there were any at all), that there were dangers to the priests through the presence of hostile Indians, and also that the climate was often unforgiving. As a rule, priests who went to visit the missions did not return home for two to three months. These trips could not be made all that often, and the priest could never visit with all his parish members. In addition, there were sick calls. It was not uncommon to ride hundred miles by horse to answer such a sick call, which quite often took one week to complete. Many parishioners saw and talked to the priest perhaps only once a year, and could only listen to mass or receive the sacraments once a year.

Yet the Mexicans remained devoted to the Catholic faith and much of the credit for that has to be given to the Penitentes. Most likely during the Mexican period the Penitentes had no so-called Moradas but used Catholic chapels, or where not available, they met privately where then the traveling priest on his mission trip read mass. The Penitentes' exercises were not at all secret, everybody could participate. Since priests so rarely visited in the missions, the Penitentes took it upon themselves to observe the religious holidays; not only the Sundays but also the name days of famous saints. Still today, many villages and pueblos observe saints holidays that have never been required by the church. It was not allowed to work on these days.

For example, the celebration of Santa Rosa was considered Embudo's main festival where until most recently mass was read in Embudo on that day. The day of Santa Rosa was considered the most religious holiday in Embudo and its rites originated in earlier times. Whenever a chapel was built, all the people of the village considered themselves the slaves of the saint after whom the chapel was named. Esclavos de San Antonio were those who belonged, for instance, to the chapel erected in honor of St. Antonio.

Every year festivities in honor of the protective patron were held, as was common in the Catholic Church. Since the priest could not care for all these distant chapels personally, annually he appointed two men and two women, usually husband and wife or brother and sister, in whose care he entrusted the chapel. Every year new men and women were chosen for this honorable office. Those entrusted with this office were called Majordomos. In individual cases Majordomos were subordinated to a so-called Syndico, which administrated the church's properties.

In those days churches often received gifts in the form of land properties, which over time were lost again. Written documentations of land transfers were basically unknown. It was enough to announce orally that this or that piece of land belonged to the church and the profits to be used for maintenance of church or toward the priest's living expenses. Over the years those oral contracts could not be enforced anymore.

The Majordomos took over their office on the patron's day and turned it over the following year to their successors. The patron saint's festivities afforded a lot of preparations. The chapel was renovated inside and outside and the altar decorated with flowers and wreaths. The patron of the chapel was given a special place on the small altar in the center of the chapel. The Majordomos were seated in front of the Saint during service. Each of the Majordomos had to hold a candle. Before the festivities began, the Majordomos started a collection and walked from house to house, or at least to those houses whose occupants were considered slaves of that particular saint. From the proceeds the costs of the festivities were covered including the expenses of the priest and the orchestra which played during the afternoon and evening events. It is known that in those days great festivals were arranged.

The most important person was the priest. Without a priest the event was a disappointment for the public. But when a priest came happiness swelled: "Ya llego el Padre." The news spread quickly. The priest stayed with the Majordomos after a long and tiring journey on horseback; they took care of priest and horse. Only the best food for the priest: frijoles with Chili and Tortillas, a meal which still today is served to welcome the priest after a long trip. The entire village was excited; everyone wanted to see the padre, wanted to kiss his hand. News was exchanged, the state of the growing season was discussed widely, and who had died in the other missions since the last visit; and last but not least the weather.

Now it was about time to go to the chapel. The children had to be ready. Religious instructions were given over the year by their fathers and mothers. Many wanted to receive their first communion during these festivities. Confessions by children and adults were heard. By now it was evening. At six o'clock the bell was ringing for the first time; the bell which, if it could talk, would have told about the sacrifices people make in this village. The best and most precious jewelries were melted into the metal of this bell. At seven o'clock everybody was present. The chapel, festively decorated was surrounded by so-called luminarias, wooden log piles, which were lit just before the evening procession. On the roof of the chapel next to the bell the Campanero was waiting with a stone in his hand. With this stone he hit the bell, which in slow or fast speed according to the Campanero's rhythm, echoed its voice.

In front of the chapel's entrance were half a dozen men assembled carrying old shot guns and with each ring of the bell shoot off their muskets. They were guns like those Billy the Kid used to have. In the chapel the priest was ready to begin the Vespers. After each Gloria Patri the bell rang and the volleys of the muskets roared. Immediately after the Vespers the procession set into motion. At first the luminarias were lit. In front, the cross lead the way, followed by two musicians with violin and guitar, then the Majordomos with the patron saint, and closing the procession were long rows of believers—children, women, and men. The bright flames illuminated the evening announcing that the festivities are in full swing. Singing the Ave Maria "Dios te salve, Maria" the procession moved slowly through the night. This procession ended the first part of the celebrations—but not for the priest who still had chores that kept him busy until deep into the night.

Early in the morning people arrived again at church to wait until mass begins at nine o'clock. If no cantor was available, the priest was singing the mass by himself. Still, it was better with a cantor and it was preferred by the parishioners. And if violin and guitar were available, then it was una misa muy bonita. During the sermon everybody was eagerly listening, even if it took an hour or longer. It was so seldom that the people could hear the Lord's word directly from the priest's mouth. Once the mass was over, the procession moved out, like on the evening before. Only this time there were no luminarias necessary because the rays of another, much stronger light made by God's hands, illuminated the worshippers. Once everybody returned to the chapel, the priest sang the oration of the day to honor the saint in front of the Holy Statue and thanked everybody, particularly the Majordomos. New Majordomos were appointed for the coming year, and with a brief reminder to take good care of the chapel, the church festivities came to an end. The priest soon said his good-byes to continue his journey to other missions, where possibly another patron fest might have been celebrated.

The festivities in the village, however, continued. Usually the majordomos organized a celebration to which the entire village was invited, and the best food that could decorate a Mexican table were served: Chicken, a deer from the near-by mountains—oh, how well this all tasted. The musicos are busy all day long. They entertain during the meal and then entertained for an hour at a dance. At three o'clock the old majordomos and other participants again gathered in the chapel. They handed over the Santo statue and the keys to the chapel to the newly appointed majordomos and afterwards a rosary was being said saying Thanks. Toward the evening the big dance began, and when the guests had enough—the fiesta was over.

Now, what did all this have to do with the Penitentes? Directly—nothing, but it showed how Mexicans in those days maintained their religion despite the rare visits by priests. After the festivities, the people were again for months at a time alone, and yet all the church holidays were observed. When lent arrived, everybody tried to maintain it according to church rules. Naturally, it was the priests who made sure that the people had opportunities to attend mass at their own chapels, and during the fast, the priest visited the big missions for two to three days while the smaller ones had to be content with one day. The priest used to travel from one mission to the next and occasionally only spent the last days of Holy Week in his own parish church. Everybody had to be given the opportunity to fulfill the duties of the church, and still today priests travel from one mission to the next, even if on a smaller scale. Parishes, still very big and far away, are not quite comparable to missions of years past.

With such a small number of priests operating during the Mexican period, and the population's limited knowledge in religious matters it was not surprising that major errors occurred. Although steadfast in their belief in god, mistakes took place especially during Lent when interpreting the suffering of Jesus Christ. After the dissolution or decline of the Third Order of Saint Francis, former members of the Order may not have immediately given up everything, but most likely continued their penances. These penances were continued by others, and step by step, they went out of control. Presumably during that time, crucifixions occurred in some isolated villages on Good Friday. It did not happen in places where priests resided, rather, only in places that priests rarely visited. Usually, this kind of penitence occurred without the priest's knowledge, and if he found out, he explained that it was not in accordance with church rules. Yet many a former member of the Third Order thought: We know better; it has been done this way in the past. Eventually these processions occurred only in secret.

Old-timer Penitentes, who remembered their fathers' habits and traditions, told this writer of the harsh penance, especially flagellation with needle-point thorny cactus, which dug deep into the penitent's flesh. The type of penance occurring during these processions, i.e. crucifixion at Good Friday, have been mentioned in reports and are erroneously still attribute to our time. But the crucifixion was not performed with nails, as those were not known in New Mexico then. This can be safely assumed, because the old hand-made tables, chairs, etc. don't show any nails to hold the furniture together.

The individual who was crucified was placed onto a large cross, which he himself carried to the Calvario [location of crucifixion], and tied down somehow with ropes, which perhaps had been spun for this particular purpose on a spinning-wheel in his home. Then, the cross with its load was lowered into a deep hole so it would not tip. One can only imagine what went on, and undoubtedly now and then the person tied to the cross was later taken off—dead.

All in all, one should not attribute these occurrences to religious fanaticism even though this behavior may have appeared as such. People without any ordinary priestly influence and paired with ignorance in religious discipline, yet steadfast in their faith, could easily fall for these aberrations. Once, then, caught up in these errors and deeply convinced to be right, it has to be difficult to give up these exercises and abruptly end them. If crucifixions were still to appear today, then it has to be considered as religious fanaticism, insubordination, and insanity. But it is now non-existent; these kinds of crucifixions belong to the past.

Were the Penitentes of that period also politically active? When the Spanish clerics were expelled, shortly after the revolution under [Guadalupe] Hidalgo, they were replaced by Mexican priests. The flame of the revolution radiated from the heart of Mexico more and more to the outer borders of the new country. The priests in those days were probably the first ones to understand the political situation in New Mexico and preferred an independent Mexico to a dependent Spanish colony.

This is only natural. Love for an independent fatherland is in one's blood, especially the Mexicans' blood. The entire history of Mexico shows that every Mexican is a politician and entrenched in modern-day revolutions. If revolutions don't proceed peacefully, then they have to be carried out with knifes and pistols. Politics and religion are the main aspects of human life in any nation, and therefore no nation can be overly condemned. It is a natural evolution in human life. Passion creates passion, and the evil of revolution can only be suffocated when the wickedness of passion has been defeated.

In the following, like in the beginning of this chapter, the author relies on the book The Soldiers of the Cross by Archbishop J. B. Salpointe. On 27 September 1821, Mexico gained its independence from Spain. Guadalupe Hidalgo, a Catholic priest, initiated this movement in 1810. On 21 May 1822, [Augustin de] Iturbide was crowned emperor of Mexico in the cathedral of Mexico City.

> [Original in English] At the end of the Pontifical Mass and of the consecration the Bishop exclaimed: "Vivat Imperator, vivat in aeternum." "Long live the Emperor," which was echoed by the audience in the words: "Vivan por muchos años el Emperdaor y las Emperatriz." (Salpointe, p. 156)

Augustin Itubide did not remain emperor for very long. He was deposed by the Mexican congress, and given a pension of $25,000 under the condition that he would leave Mexico and settle in Italy, which he did.

> This took place in the beginning of May 1823. From Livorno (Italy) where the Emperor had taken his residence, he went to England in January 1824, where he heard that a revolution was prepared in Spain against Mexico. This he wrote to the Mexican congress offering at the same time his services for the protection of his country. The answer was not only a refusal of the offer, but a decree by which Iturbide was declared an outlaw. In his anxiety to find an opportunity to exert his natural activity and perhaps trusting that his countrymen would call on him again to take the reins of government, he started at once, without waiting for an answer to his letter, and reached the port of Soto La Marina on the 14th of May, 1824. There he was apprised by General Garza that he was proscribed and on the 17th, was notified by an adjutant that he should prepare for death, as he was to be shot at three o'clock of the same day. Without showing any emotion, Iturbide replied: "Tell General Garza that I am ready

to die, if he only gives me three days to make my peace with God." (Salpointe, p. 158)

The Archbishop continues:

> H. H. Bancroft (Historia de Mexico) from whom we have taken our information about the fall of the Mexican empire, does not state whether the short delay asked for by the doomed great patriot was accorded to him or not, but be this as it may, it is well known that the Emperor submitted to the unmerited sentence and died like a brave soldier and a good Christian.

On 4 October 1824 the constitution of the new republic was announced: La Republica Federal de Los Estados Unidos de Mexico. During this time the church wasn't hurting, "[Original in English] except from the revolutions which alienated from her many influential citizens by placing them in contact with part leaders connected with the lodges." (Salpointe, p. 159)

In 1826 the Vicar General of the diocese of Durango, Don Augustin Fernandez, made a Visita Pastoral to New Mexico, especially Santa Fe. The only aspect known about the political activities of the Penitentes in those days, that this writer could find, is again contained in the book Soldiers of the Cross.

> [Peter Küppers cites verbatim nearly three pages (pp. 161-163) from Salpointe's chapter "Republica de Mexico" describing the history and culture of the Penitentes—not reproduced here.]

In 1824 New Mexico became [Mexican] territory and Antonio Narbona its first governor, who in turn was succeeded in 1827 by Manuel Armijo.[1] The following year, 1828, José Antonio Chavez became governor. As a result of political activities hostile toward the church, most Spanish priests left New Mexico, and it was difficult to find immediate replacements for them. For the new priests, it was a harsh undertaking, since none of them was acquainted with the territory of New Mexico. Still, there were priests like Rev. Juan Felipe Ortiz, who was born in New Mexico, and who in 1832 became Vicar General Forane.[2]

It was the time of decadence among the brotherhoods of the Penitentes.

Politics played the main role in the clerical decline, followed by the evictions or forced departure of the Spanish priests as well as the Franciscans who were well acquainted with the colonization of New Mexico. Each political disorder, generally, brings along a struggle against the church and all segments of society are pulled into this misery. It is easy to understand, that political leaders also pulled the Penitentes into this chaos. But the limited number of priests, then, had little opportunity to influence the situation.

What were conditions after the United States annexed the territory? Through the Treaty of Guadalupe Hidalgo in 1848, New Mexico became part of the United States. Religious conditions in New Mexico remained the same, but as mentioned before, many Mexican priests left New Mexico to return to Mexico. In 1850 during the papacy of Pius IX, New Mexico became a Vicariate Apostolic and Rev. Juan Baptiste Lamy its Vicar.

Father Lamy was born on 11 October 1814 in Lempdes, in the Diocese of Clermont, France. Ordained in 1838, he arrived in Cincinnati, Ohio the following year to assist Bishop Purcell. It is common knowledge that when he arrived in Santa Fe after a several months-long journey, he learned that nobody knew of his appointment as the new apostolic vicar. Even the Bishop of Durango, who had jurisdiction over Santa Fe, was not informed, and so it happened that his appointment found little response in Santa Fe. The newly appointed Vicar Apostolic was forced to travel on horse-back to Durango, Mexico, which again took a few months, in order to present his appointment papers from the Pope. Then he returned to Santa Fe. In the meantime he left his companion Father Joseph P. Machebeuf in Santa Fe. Archbishop Salpointe reported about the situation:

> [Original in English] He left in Santa Fe the Rev. Joseph P. Machebeuf who had come with him from Ohio for the Missions of New Mexico. The Rev. gentleman was invited by the parish priest of Santa Fe, Rev. Lujan, to sing mass on the next Sunday and tried to address the congregation after the priest had introduced him not at all very warmly. It must be taken as a matter of course that the new missionary spoke good words for the glory of God and in behalf of his Bishop, but the fact is that nobody understood much of what he said, as he did not speak the language of the country. Hence it was that a controversy arose among the people on the plaza, after mass, as to what religion the stranger might belong to. "He must

be a Jew or a Protestant," said some, "because he does not speak as Christians do." "Quien sabe" (Who can tell), replied others. "Still he said mass in Latin, and like a priest who knows how to do it, and be it said en passant, he sings better than our priests." At last, a good woman, who like other women, always anxious to know what is the matter, had stopped and listened to the running conversation, stepped bravely forward and pertinently said: "What reason have you to be perplexed about the religion of this man? Did he not give a proof that he is a Catholic by the way he made the sign of the cross before giving the sermon?" This sensible remark ended the question and removed great suspicions in regard to the religion of the Rev. Joseph P. Machebeuf. (pp. 196-97)

From this little story, it is easy to recognize, how difficult it was for new missionaries to communicate with the people. "They did not speak the language of Christians," was the opinion of Santa Fe churchgoers. From the beginning, the situation was very complicated to establish clerical authority, and that is particularly applicable to the Penitentes of the time.

Despite the poor conditions of the church and despite the small number of priests, the now Spanish Americans lived a good Christian life. To make that point, Archbishop Salpointe says the following:

The writer of these pages [Salpointe], who came to New Mexico nine years after Bishop Lamy, remembers yet with pleasure and edification, the Christian customs he noticed in existence in many of the Mexican families, where he had occasionally to stop, when visiting the scattered towns and settlements of his parish. In the first place, prayers and catechism were taught orally to the young children by some member of the family or by some trusty person of the neighborhood and repeated word for word, question after question until some part of the lesson would remain in the memory of the hearers. This was hard work, but a meritorious one and one of great value to the missionary, who had only to explain the mysteries and the chief points of our religion to the children thus instructed at home, when he had to prepare them for their first Holy Communion. This teaching is now mostly left to the parochial schools, where they exist, but at the time we refer to there were no parochial schools except in the City of Santa Fe, and in our opinion, these schools can accomplish very little in inculcating religion in the hearts of the young, if this work has not been commenced at home. (p. 199)

The Venerable Archbishop continues:

> Every evening it was customary to make the children say some prayers which always terminated with the words: Bendito y alabado sea el Santisimo Sacramento del Altar—Blessed and hallowed be the Most Holy Sacrament of the Altar. After this the innocent creatures, still kneeling, had to kiss the hand of their parents and receive their blessing before going to bed. The same blessing has also to be asked even by the grown children of the house, when they were coming from their own confession. (pp.199-200)
> (…)
> Another kind (continues the Archbishop in his book) of a pious and interesting salutation was used by persons at a distance from each other. The one who could first address the other by the words: "Ave Maria" had the right to be answered by the recitation of the whole Hail Mary, for his intention. These and many other manifestations of a Christian spirit were very common among the people of New Mexico, when Bishop Lamy took possession of his Vicariate. (p. 200)

This proves the existence of a good faith among the people in those days. And one has to include the Penitentes. The conclusion needs to be drawn, that all religious exercises were done in good faith, even those which were done during the Fast.

In 1853, Santa Fe was elevated to a diocese. And only two years after his appointment to Vicar Apostolic, Bishop Lamy became its first residing bishop. Then, only ten priests were residing in New Mexico. Archbishop Salpointe lists them:

Jose Manuel Gallegos
Jose de Jesus Leiva

Luvero
Jose de Jesus Lujan
Antonio de Jesus Martinez
Vicente Montano
Fernando Ortiz
Juan Felipe Ortiz
Ramon Salazar
Juan Trujillo

With this small number of priests Bishop Lamy began to manage his huge diocese. The conditions in it were very poor and he was confronted with the biggest task that a prelate of the church had ever faced.

One of Bishop Lamy's tasks was to regulate the Penitente brotherhoods. Initially there was little to do as there were too few priests to cover so large an area and the political turmoil deemed any improvement impossible. Also, the first Archbishop's nationality has to be considered. Lamy was well aware of the fact that the people of Mexican descent were accustomed to a Mexican government.

There was no other option than to hire more priests for the diocese. In 1859 the number of parishes with residing priests climbed to eighteen. During the tenure of the first three bishops, 83 priests came to New Mexico. Most of them arrived from France—pioneers in New Mexico—who in the true spirit of religion led a harsh missionary life. During the tenure of Archbishop Chapelle [1894–1897] 22 priests arrived; among them eighteen French men, three Germans, and one Dutch. This opened the door to improve missionary work in New Mexico.

The Archbishops and the priests obviously directed some of their attention toward the Penitentes. Once Archbishop Salpointe observed and studied the Penitentes, he began step by step to eradicate years of neglect that led to the unrestrained behavior. On more than one occasion, Archbishop Salpointe wrote to the various moradas requesting obedience to the Catholic Church. He, as well as the priests who were supposed to initiate change, experienced stiff resistance. Many moradas became defiant and uncooperative. Still, he initiated the rules, the Penitentes use today. The acceptance of the Penitentes brotherhood by the Catholic Church is dependent on the adherence to these rules. The church's main concern was to remain unwavering in its prohibition of public flagellations. Therefore, one cannot accuse the Church of negligence in educating the Penitentes in the spirit of the Church. Yet still today, uninformed observers blame the Church that it tolerates the Penitentes' public activities. This is not true and does not do justice to the efforts of the church.

It was nearly impossible to enforce obedience, as the aberrations were so deeply rooted. Still, the Penitentes distanced themselves more and more from the public sphere, exercised their penances in the moradas or, under the protection of darkness, in the mountains and arroyos. Archbishop Salpointe even prohibited the Holy Sacraments for those Penitentes who publicly performed these senseless penances. This resulted in a situation often difficult and uncomfortable for the priest. If he refused absolution, he alone was blamed and many a priest endured the anger [of family members and/or other Penitentes]. It is wrong, however, to assume that all Penitentes were involved. Many moradas obeyed the law of the church.

For those retaining the practices, the situation only changed slowly. In an effort by the Penitentes to regain the Holy Sacraments, the exercises disappeared little by little from the public sphere to be secretively maintained in many moradas. The reason why many did not obey the rules of the Church can be attributed to a certain fanaticism. There were even moradas that considered themselves higher than the Church. The influence of political leaders may also have played a role.

If, for instance, the priest's mass and the Penitentes' gathering in the morada conflicted, it was often the morada, and not the church, that was visited. During Holy Week, instead of attending the holiest ceremonies of the church, the Penitentes often remained day and night in the morada to proceed with their own exercises. The local priest with considerable prudence and diplomacy could slowly change this behavior. It was for the good of the Penitentes when Archbishop Salpointe ordered that only those may belong to a morada who fulfill their Easter duties. Those who disobeyed could no longer be a member of the Catholic Church.

Some poems of the time show, that the brotherhood lost a lot of its respect:

Penitente Pecador
Porque te andas azotando
Por una vaca que robe
Y aqui la ando disquitando

Penitent sinner
Why do you flagellate
For a cow I stole
Here I'll pay

Perhaps, characters were admitted to the brotherhoods that shouldn't have been, because of their aggravating life styles. There is no doubt that the brotherhoods deviated [from the Catholic norm] because, year after year, there were not enough honorable leaders available who could have or would have provided religious leadership. People were accepted who might have been in need of political or judicial protection. Past times explain a lot.

Without a doubt, the situation slowly changed for the better. First, the clerical authority was unforgiving in its application of disciplinary procedures against those who did not obey church laws. Second, good Penitentes realized that the continuation of their brotherhoods would become impossible if they did not obey the church. For years now, the Penitentes have moved closer and closer to the church and yet at the same time the brotherhoods have retreated into their moradas. Still today a few individual moradas offer public spectacles particularly during the fast. Those then are being censured by the Church.

This writer worked for years in areas of New Mexico with many Penitentes and he admits that the Penitentes are among his best friends, but more importantly, the same Penitentes listen to his concerns and follow his advice. Today, the Catholic Church in New Mexico would be in higher esteem among Spanish Americans, if more Penitentes belonged to the moradas, practicing in accordance with the rules and regulations of the Church.

One will never find a Penitente who would send his child to a protestant school. He would rather not have his child receive any school education before exposing him or her to the dangers of a Protestant education. The Protestant schools in New Mexico are the main reason why the Catholic faith of Spanish Americans is dropping. These schools take away from them the most precious gift that they own—their religion. But Protestantism cannot replace the loss as it does not offer anything better. Protestantism poisons the soul of the Spanish Americans. Eventually, this will lead to disappointment and result in the rise of other religions. When the religious structure has been taken away, Spanish Americans will regress. In many places where there are no Penitentes anymore, the Protestant schools quickly indoctrinate the Catholic youth; yet, in places where strong moradas are still in existence, Protestantism cannot permanently infiltrate. Because of the Penitentes' faith, the Catholic religion remains strong in those places, because no children of a Penitente will ever attend a school that endangers their religion.

Protestantism is quite a different issue in New Mexico than in most other states. It is strange how Protestantism progresses among so many Spanish Americans. Protestant schools can be found in many Spanish settlements. The best families are sought out and under the pretense that the children are free to practice their religion, fathers and mothers are persuaded to send their children to the Protestant schools. When parents find out later that the children are educated according to Protestant conventions, they do not have the stamina to pull them out of school. The best pupils then are persuaded to continue their studies in order to function later as predicadores [preachers] and ministers among their own people. It is not a rare occurrence to find such Protestant ministers in the resolana, talking about religion, priests, etc. in the shade of a tree or an adobe building: "Gutta caveat lapidem, non vi sed saepe cadendo"—a constant drip will eat the stone. Those ministers consider it their duty to visit Catholic families and hand out free bibles. The bible is the key along with how the minister interprets the bible: "Yo lo se; yo soy uno de ustedes" (I know best, because I am one of you).

During Lent there will be usually a special Protestant mission. Two to six ministers will come to the village in which the mission is held. That impresses the locals. What kind of means the ministers use will be illustrated in the following, true event. Some years ago, a Colorado minister came to visit the Peñasco parish. First he visited Embudo or Dixon. The [Catholic] priest ignored his presence until this minister identified himself as an ex-priest. His name was Rodriguez. When he criticized religion, priests, and nuns a bit too much the situation became uncomfortable. He even criticized the Penitentes publicly in his frequent evening gatherings.

The priest [likely Peter Küppers himself] called on four good Penitentes and asked them to attend the instructional evenings of the Protestant church and report back to him. To his own detriment, the so-called ex-priest talked about Penitentes. After the celebrations were over and the gentleman retired to the house of the residing minister, the Penitentes followed him to his house and approached him. In no uncertain terms, they made it clear that he had no right to publicly talk about the Penitentes, let alone to criticize them, and that in the event of a recurrence something unpleasant might happen to him. The minister was easily hoodwinked, and from this point on he was suspicious of the Penitentes. Eventually, this self-styled ex-priest moved his work to other missions in the Parish of Peñasco.

At the same time, a Catholic missionary worked in the missions. His name was Rev. Zuniga. Just like the priest, the missionary was not too much bothered by the ex-priest until the gentleman's business became too controversial. Then, suddenly, the ex-priest disappeared. It was a known fact that the missionary and the priest asked the gentleman to attend a little get-together, but as soon as he sensed danger, he was gone for good. This, however, was not good enough for a so-called Predicador. He paid the priest a visit and asked if one of us was willing to attend a public discussion with the ex-priest?

"Certainly we will, whenever it is convenient!"

"Well," the Predicador replied, "then the ex-priest has to come back and face the music." A few days later, a committee from the protestant church arrived to work out details for the discussion. A topic of discussion was arranged and even a date was set. The priest hurried to get the permission from the archbishop, which was granted. Father Zuniga took on the position of commentator.

A few days prior to the debate, again a committee from the Protestant church appeared. An old Ford stopped in front of the presbytery and soon the passengers sat in the office of the priest. The priest had no idea that the so-called ex-priest was still in the Ford, afraid to come in. To his surprise, the leader of the committee contended that the ex-priest seemed to be in some danger if he attend a public discussion in Peñasco and that Embudo would be a better place to conduct the debate. A significant number of Protestants lived there.

> "Gentlemen," the priest replied, "there is no danger at all for the ex-priest. Besides, more people are living in Peñasco than in Embudo as it is the center of the parish and it's easier for parishioners from the missions to attend in Peñasco. Mr. Rodriguez should not fear. Nothing will happen to him. I will take personal responsibility for his safety."

This did not put them at ease. The priest was asked to provide a written guarantee that nothing will happen to the ex-priest and that he will come away unharmed. A document was drafted making the priest of Peñasco responsible for the safety of the ex-priest during the discussion in the hall. After the document was signed, the priest regretted to have taken on this responsibility but now it was a done deal.

The priest was convinced that on 1 April [1926], a large crowd will gather to attend the debate, not only Catholics, but also Spanish American protestants. While Father Zuniga prepared for the debate, the priest wondered how to keep order in the hall, especially since the mood seemed to take a rather threatening character? He thought of his Penitentes. They wouldn't betray their priest but comply with his request. Every section of the Penitentes was notified that the Hermano Major with three selected Penitentes was to come to the presbytery to accept instructions from the priest.

"Señores, on the first of April, I must have about forty Penitentes to my absolute disposal. They will sit in the front row during the debate. Father Zuniga will take his seat to my left and the ex-priest Rodriguez as the guest to my right. My orders have to be followed without hesitation. In the event that I lose control, it is for you to follow my orders to protect the ex-priest. The other Penitentes have to be there as well, but distributed across the hall—one here, another one there, in the event of a tumult.

The deal was done and the priest relaxed.

The day of the event neared. Five minutes before one o'clock Father Zuniga and the priest entered the hall. Never have there been more people in Peñasco than on that day. The hall was filled with curiosity seekers and for many it was standing room only. People from all missions were represented. Father Zuniga and a companion took their seats. Across from the priests sat forty Penitentes, ready for any emergency.

Father Küppers and the sisters often built and repaired parish buildings themselves, like this building in the Peñasco-Dixon parish (ca. 1925). Courtesty Historic-Artistic Patrimony and Archives, Archdiocese of Santa Fe.

At one o'clock sharp, the ex-priest entered accompanied by three ministers or predicadores. After a short nervous greeting, the show began under the auspices of the priest. The priest informed the audience to remain quiet and reminded them that he was responsible for the ex-priest's safety. Father Zuniga and the ex-priest were introduced. The latter had a little boy along with him who may have been ten or eleven years old. Most of the audience knew why he took the boy on his apostolic and rather aggravating propaganda tours and felt pity for the boy.

All were ready for every eventuality and for every accusation: Anti-Catholic propaganda against priests and nuns. Unfortunately, he was in the wrong place in Peñasco. Father Zuniga had to present his papers, provide his curriculum vitae, and proof of their authenticity, which was naturally no problem. Then it was the suspicious ex-priest's turn, who explained that he did not bring his papers and could therefore not present any proof of authenticity of his career.

"Then give us a run-down of your career as good as possible."
The priests understood immediately that a few things were not proper and were soon convinced that the man had never been a priest. When he was done, he was informed that his statement was politely accepted, even though it was not quite satisfactory.

Now the debate began. Rodriguez first elaborated about his thesis, but did not leave a noticeable impression, and at the end of his reasoning, nobody knew anymore what he was talking about. Father Zuniga proved his thesis in perfect Spanish. Then he turned the tables and cornered the guy so tightly that people on several occasions laughed aloud. The poor sucker was so embarrassed that he called the Indians in the audience 'uneducated.' The talk was interrupted only once by a Protestant schoolteacher who was not of Spanish blood (the teacher, incidentally, converted to the Catholic faith when he was on his death bed).

The mood turned threatening and a nod toward the Penitentes would have ended the debate. The priest had to intervene—the Penitentes were ready. A request for order was issued. Then Father Zuniga was asked to give a short history of the Catholic Church and to remind everybody that among thousands of priests perhaps one can be found who does injustice to his high position and brings confusion to the people. We won.

The debate itself did not take long because the defeat of Protestantism was obvious. Longer was Father Zuniga's speech, which he directed toward the representative of Protestantism:

Señor, everyone is convinced that you lost the debate. So please accept the following advice: It does not pay for you or for any other man to spread anti-Catholic propaganda among the Spanish Americans. In the past you might have been more successful; today not anymore. Have a good day and please leave Peñasco—and don't come back

Under the cheers of the people the priests left the hall thinking that Rodriguez would follow. When the men stepped out in the open air, they heard growing tumult in the hall and the priest made his way back in. To the priest's great surprise, the Penitentes had the man circled and the Hermano Major advised him never to return to Peñasco to spread his propaganda and to remember that there are many means to prevent such propaganda. The Penitentes were admonished to let the man go immediately. The priest saw him enter his car to Embudo from where he secretly took the train the following day. None of the remaining ministers said a word. This memorable day is still today remembered on the missions of Peñasco—and is still in the minds of the ministers. On this day the biggest propaganda was broken up.

The Penitentes of Today

Before this writer will discuss the internal structure of the Penitentes, it is appropriate to address the current state of the brotherhoods. One must differentiate among the Penitentes. The true Penitentes are those who worship in accordance with the rules of the Catholic Church and most brotherhoods have, indeed, accepted the Catholic Church. Unfortunately there are still a few Penitentes organizations, which are not acknowledged by the Catholic Church because of their public and fanatic acts of penance and the subsequent nuisances; but also because they accept members who are a detriment to the community. These brotherhoods consider the Church generally secondary and place themselves above the Church. Some time ago a non-Catholic told the following story:

> Last year during Holy Week, I drove to Santa Fe. Along the road, some thirty miles north of Santa Fe, I saw several cars parked. It was during Lent. The passengers left their cars behind, and my first thought was that there was a football game or alike under way. Since I am always attracted to sport events, I wanted to know more. Looking closer, I discovered several groups of men and women walking through the prairie. Some were using binoculars and appeared to scan the area for something. My curiosity awakened, I joined one group which told me why they were here: The Penitentes were soon to appear in their procession. It did not take long when we saw them in the distance. It was a small group of Penitentes. Each of the three of the brothers carried a big, heavy cross on their exposed shoulders and backs, which I would not want to carry for even five minutes. Two Penitentes each helped the cross carriers along with a whip. Nobody else participated in the procession. Slowly, the cross carriers inched their way to the morada. All visitors could observe the event undisturbed. When the Penitentes disappeared into the Morada, some

spectators dared to walk up to the entrance and were admitted. What may have happened inside, I do not know, because this event turned me off so much so that I returned to my car and drove away.

"So, this still happens today," the man continues, "in the Catholic Church, and the priests, whom I consider well educated, allow these kinds of events. What do you have to say, Father?"

The answer was that the Catholic Church and its priests have nothing to do with these events, and that they do not tolerate this sort of fanaticism. For instance four years ago, the late Archbishop of Santa Fe, His Excellency, the Most Rev. A. T. Daeger [1919–1932] prohibited in no uncertain terms these displays, and repeated what other Archbishops of Santa Fe had done before him, namely to punish such moradas with an interdict.

Although this changed the man's attitude, he could not resist remarking that these few moradas are the causes for the random condemnation of all moradas, and make Anglos consider the Catholic Church in New Mexico as medieval. However, the use of the word "medieval" may not be appropriate considering what the church has accomplished over the centuries. In the Medieval Ages the Church was as fresh and blossoming as it is today.

True, moradas that position themselves above the Church and its priests are still a nuisance today. Members of such moradas do not consider it a clerical order to attend mass on Sundays or to participate in the church festivities during Lent. No, first the morada—then the Church, and during a year the Church does not see any of them. These are not Penitentes but disobedient, self-styled Catholics.

It is a peculiar characteristic of those moradas to admit visitors for a charge, so that the imitation of Christ's suffering appears more like a theater play. It has been said that the proprietor of a certain spa invited guests from the East during Lent with the advertisement that they could attend all ceremonies of the Penitentes. The informant further added that the proprietor of the convalescence home or the spa agreed with the Penitentes to have them admitted for one dollar each. The fact is that each year during Lent certain moradas attract curious tourists and it should be pointed out that Penitentes who make a public spectacle of their moradas are no Penitentes.

The Church does not recognize those Penitentes who place their own rituals above the ceremonies and culture of the Church. A priest once pointed out, when he visits a certain area in his parish during Lent, the Penitentes there do not visit the church or even attend mass, but instead perform their own rituals in the morada and sometimes even in public. The necessary response is to prevent these people from receiving the sacraments unless they have been informed of their clerical duties. These Penitentes conduct severe penances; however, no case is known in which an actual crucifixion has been performed.

It does not bother the Church when Penitentes roam the mountains in the daytime or at night, sing their own particular songs and hymns, and perform minor penances as long as they are not a public nuisance. This happens in quite a few places. Even what happens inside the moradas is nobody's business, as long as nothing offensive happens.

A procession in harmony with Church rules is actually very nice. Quite often at night during Lent the priest stands in front of his house facing the nearby mountains where the movement of the lanterns indicates the direction of the procession. And sometimes, one can listen to the songs of the Penitentes—first in the distance, then closer and closer until they fade again into the distance.

This is a piece of New Mexico's history and tradition. Three years ago this writer was fortunate to observe a procession of the Penitentes on the eve of Ash Wednesday. Toward nine o'clock in the evening he heard their songs, stepped immediately outside and sought cover in the darkness of the church so not be detected. An impressive procession of men neared the church. Two men carried crosses and in two orderly rows the other Penitentes followed, some carrying lanterns. Next to the church, a crucifixion scene was set up and all said some prayers in front of it. The men who carried the crosses put them down and everyone entered the church to pray for about half an hour. As soon as the procession left the church, and the two men shouldered their crosses, the priest stepped forward to talk to them.

This was in Peñasco and nobody could voice any objection to this procession. If everybody remembered the Passion during Holy Week, as the Penitentes did that evening, it would be encouraging. The priest reminded his Penitentes to come early to church tomorrow morning and if possible, to receive the Holy Communion. He added, "I am happy; in the eyes of God it is certainly pleasant to celebrate Holy Week instead of forgetting Christ or even to sin." In a few minutes, the procession disappeared into the mountains to their morada. The Church has no objections against such processions and demonstrations by the Penitentes. They are displayed today by Penitentes in front of their moradas and they are in harmony with Church rules.

The priest will enter these moradas at any time, either to attend their ceremonies or to pay a special visit. The Penitentes are happy when the priest honors them with his visit and willingly accept advice. He insists that the rules of the morada are carefully followed, and that no member is admitted whose behavior is known to be improper. Those unworthy of the membership in the brotherhood, have to leave. Last year, eight members of a morada were dismissed because they did not follow Church rules and ordinances. These dismissals, though, carried the great danger of discord; yet it is better to remove all dubious elements from the morada than to fight those disobeying clerical rules. And it happens that dismissed members organize another brotherhood in which case those people fall into the same class mentioned in the beginning of this chapter.

There are moradas that exist individually, which has the advantage of self-government with guidance from a priest. The Morada de Los Salazares or the Morada de Arriba in Embudo are, for instance, such self-governing moradas. Other moradas have special organizational structures and are incorporated. About ten to twenty moradas have a main morada or Centro with special committee members, and the subordinate moradas are controlled and governed by the main morada. The Centro owns a special banner and during every Lent period its representatives visit the secondary moradas. This visit is official and is called "mission." In the past, the Hermano del Centro was such an important personality that he considered himself as the bishop of the Penitentes. Those times are long gone. The visits of the Hermano del Centro and his adjutants are serious matters. Their efforts are to stamp out possible reoccurring wrong-doings, and to reaffirm the Church rules among the members.

During one of his visits the priest will celebrate mass for all members the Centro's moradas and use the opportunity to instruct the members. If there are difficulties among the members that cannot be solved by the Centro or even by the Hermano Major, it is up to the priest to make a decision. Under the penalty of expulsion this decision had to be followed. So, the priest has to act carefully otherwise he might lose members.

For instance, a Penitente who belonged to the morada for years was left by his legal wife. Since it was not his fault and the wife requested a divorce, the man could remain a member of the morada. A few years later, however, he married again in a civil ceremony. Through this step then he could no longer belong to the morada. This case was presented to the priest for decision, and after serious deliberation, showing some leniency, the priest announced the following decision:

Since the man has served his church faithfully for years, he will be permitted to say his prayers alone under the exclusion of the public in the morada; however, he is under no circumstances allowed to accept a position in the brotherhood.

All Penitentes were asked to pray that his first marriage would soon be back in order. This decision found little support among the Penitentes and eventually the priest had to apply the rules, literally suspending the man from his morada. The priest's first decision showed mercy but the observance of the rules generally gives the best results, as this case proved over time.

One of the rules for moradas is that the priest will make final decisions in difficult circumstances that cannot be resolved among Penitentes. For instance, the member of a certain morada, which is subordinate to the main morada of Taos, could no longer be considered a member in good standing. His revenge lead to one difficulty after another until the priest finally had to come to a decision.

[Peter Küppers's recollections of the letter are poor and so was his Spanish. Here is a loose translation.]

> Office of the Hermano Major del Centro
> Taos N.M. May 31, 1933
>
> Rev. Father:
>
> Health, Peace, and Thanks, we give you in the name of our Lord Jesus Christ.
>
> Honorable Father: We, the members of the pious fraternity of Nuestro Padre Jesus Nazareno, incorporated as El Centro, and as officials of said association wish to give you the following information in hope that with your cooperation we can avoid a scandal—.
>
> There was a brother who belonged to a section of San—. He was expelled by the order of El Centro and other officials. Before his expulsion, they tried to reason with him during visits, but he paid no attention and refused to adhere to the rules and to cooperate. Because of his refusal to cooperate, he was excluded by the local authorities. These local officials were authorized by the General Council to maintain good order and to manage this section which belonged to El Centro.

The brother to whom we refer is Brother—. We were informed that said brother walks in scandalizing manners in public for the purpose of flagellation. He walks in the nude in public and goes to the section of San— to disturb the brothers there and **we as officials of said association do not approve of this exercise in public.** [emphasis Küppers's]

Enclosed you will find a copy of the letter which was sent to said Brother—by the Hermano Major of El Centro. Since nothing the local authorities did helps this situation, we put this affair in your hands and respectfully await your orders and hope for your blessing.

Respectfully,

Hermano Major del Centro
Councilor General
Advisor General

Testified by Seal:
Secretary of El Centro[1]

The content of this letter says that a member of the morada was suspended by the Centrum. He was accused of disreputable behavior such as public flagellation and immoral public appearance which disgraced the members of his morada, so the priest was called upon to make a decision. It is remarkable that the following statements appear in the letter:

"We, the local officials of the incorporated brotherhood prohibit such public exercises."

This by itself might already be confusing, as such exercises and excesses are equally banned in private. It becomes clear from the letter, that the priest will make the final decision if the local officials are unable or unwilling to resolve the situation.

Today, Penitentes believe that the Church comes first and the morada second. Subsequently all Penitentes appear at church events. They gather at their moradas and then proceed singing toward the church with the crucifix heading the procession. During the Lent periods the Penitentes do the fourteen Stations of the Cross in the church, and, if they want, later again in their morada.

A special day for the brotherhoods is Good Friday—in fact, it is their most important day. They have their special exercises in the morada. In the morning and early afternoon, the members attend church. The brotherhoods split into three sections. If weather conditions are poor and the Stations of the Cross cannot be done outside, the *tre ore* [Italian for "three hours" referring to the time that Christ was on the Cross on Good Friday] services are held in church. The first section of the Penitentes arrives in church around noon; the fourteen Stations of the Cross are prayed by the Penitentes and thereafter the priest will give his sermon until one o'clock. The second section appears and the procedure is repeated. At two o'clock the third and last section arrives and after the last sermon, is the worship of the Holy Cross, just like on the morning of Good Friday during service. The church is always packed with believers.

When the weather is nice and the procession can move outside, everybody gathers at one o'clock in the church, including, naturally, the Penitentes with cross and banner. All then proceed from the church to the morada: the cross, the banner, the Penitentes and the rest of the believers. The priest walks among the Penitentes. In front of the morada the cross walk begins. Thirteen small crosses in equal distance from each other are placed and at the so-called Calvario a big cross is erected. The priest performs the stations and the Penitentes sing while moving from one station to the next. At the Calvario the priest gives his sermon. Thereafter all return to the church to worship at the holy cross. It is fairly easy to arrange everything in a way that both Penitentes and non-Penitentes are happy and that everything is done in the most ecclesiastical way possible.

Are Penitentes today involved in politics? The brotherhoods that are discussed here are not at all politically active. That is not to say that Penitentes don't protect each other. But it is an unspoken rule among Penitentes, not to bring up political questions in gathering in the moradas. Attempts have been made, however, to pull the brotherhoods into politics. Most of the attempts ended dismally. Several years ago, representatives from different moradas came into the territory. Discussions were held in different moradas to join into a collective organization. Some were in favor of uniting, others were not. Subsequently, some moradas parted in discord which meant nothing less than a future of slow decline. Representatives, who appeared to be politically active, presented the situation to the priest for his decision. The priest was informed that reorganization under legal protection was necessary and that nobody would be allowed to carry the insignias of the Penitentes unless the brotherhood was incorporated. To that purpose, it was considered necessary to call a general assembly of all Penitentes in New Mexico.

"Who will head such a movement?" asked the priest.

"The man's name is Fulano Tal."

"I don't believe this man is a practicing Catholic, even though he is supposed to be a Penitente."

When he did not receive an answer, the priest continued:

"In an organization such as a tightly knit brotherhood, the risk of political influence is large, particularly when a politician wants to head this organization. I know Fulano Tal as a politician but not as a practicing Catholic, thus he is not to be tolerated in any morada, let alone be allowed to head the organization. That would indicate the break-down of the organization of Penitentes which is a direct subordinate of the church. Under those circumstances, no priest can tend to the needs of the Penitentes. Therefore, I have to prohibit my Penitentes to join this new organization."

The gentlemen were disappointed and one of them clearly stated that once the legal question had been resolved, Penitentes who had not joined the new organization, would not be allow to show the Confradia insignia any longer in public.

"You are mistaken. The Confradia de Nuestro Padre Jesus is a Church organization and as such subject to orders by the Church and particularly the priest of the parish. As long as the organization is clerical, nobody will meddle with the Church. Political questions as such are not an issue among Penitentes. Everybody steps to the ballot box and votes his political conscience."

What hurts the organization is that a Penitente can only belong to a morada but no other association. Otherwise he has to leave the morada. That is even the case when an organization includes insurance of the family. For instance, a Penitente should not belong to the K[nights] of C[olumbus]. In recent years, however, many moradas changed those rules.

It is very interesting to observe how caring Penitentes are when help is needed, particularly among their own members. If a Penitente is sick, the Hermanos take care of him. This will be done in any case, even if the Penitente is poor. Every night two members of the morada are prepared to take care of the sick. They make sure that enough fire wood is secured, groceries are available, and often take up a collection among the members of the morada to purchase other necessities. To visit the sick, is one of the main duties of a Penitente.

The death of a member or next of kin shows the extent of Christian brotherly love. In the past, it was common to not even call the priest for a funeral and instead the Penitentes, without much ado, took care of business themselves. This was changed over time with some gentle nudging. Still, the Penitentes shoulder all responsibilities. The family hands over the body of the deceased to the Penitentes. They lay out the dead, provide the casket, and hold the wake or velorio. As there are no embalmers available in the areas, the body remains only one day and one night above ground. While the body lies in state, the Penitentes alternately sing and pray. It happens that members from far-away moradas are called upon to attend the velorio. If a priest happens to be available for the funeral, the Penitentes are expected to arrange the formalities with him. The grave at the cemetery is dug by Penitentes the day of the funeral. The morning the body is taken to the church, the Penitentes lead the procession, praying and singing, followed by the body, the relatives of the deceased, and finally the other visitors.

Quite often in New Mexico one can find simple wood crosses along the way held in place with stones. Because the distance to the chapel or church is often considerable, the procession rests a few times on their way. The exact spot where the casket has been set down on the ground is then marked with stones. Later, a small cross is erected there and such a spot is called descanso or rest place. Once the procession arrives at the church, the singing of the Penitentes stops and the priest accepts the casket. If a priest cannot be present, the casket is placed in the church and a rosary is read for the deceased. The same happens at the grave site. The close of the funeral does not yet free the Penitentes of their responsibilities. If the family happens to be so poor that help is required, the Penitentes will care for the members as best as possible. This is Christian love.

The morada, or the club house if you will, is the place Penitentes meet to tend to their business. It is not true, that moradas are always built in remote, inaccessible areas. One can find moradas not only hidden far in the mountains but also close to county roads visible to everybody. It is often assumed, that moradas hide secret belongings and instruments that can never be seen by non-Penitentes.

The morada is generally a long stretched adobe building with a flat roof. The four adobe walls are much longer than wide. The roof consists of long beams which keep the walls together. On top are tightly lined saplings which in turn are covered by a six inches thick layer of soil. Over time the mud becomes so hard that only on rare occasions does rain penetrate the roof. The morada has only one entrance crowned by a small spire which contains the bell or a simple cross. The exterior walls are covered with mud, and in some cases, with white soil native to the mountains.

The interior of the morada is very simple. Upon entering the morada, visitors will see one room covering two thirds of the morada. A small window provides light. This is the chapel. There are no benches or chairs, only a crudely constructed home-made alter alongside the entire wall. The altar and the interior are absolutely spotless. The altar is covered with white linen and in the center is positioned the so-called "Sangre de Cristo." This is an old carved cross. The Christ figure, too, is woodwork. This is the symbol of the Penitentes. The carving, which is generally covered with Calico [unbleached cotton] fabric, is not particularly impressive, and yet, upon reflecting for a moment, one can recognize a living faith in it. A hundred years ago and more, there were hardly any finely carved and artistically well done statues in Mexico. All statues were hand-carved and more or less of poor quality. Despite this first un-esthetic impression, there is a certain beauty in the statues.

The name "Sangre de Cristo" has its origin in Jesus Christ's blood on the cross. This crucifix precedes any procession. Also, one can expect on the altar an often life-size carved figure, dressed in women clothes and its face covered with a black scarf during the last three days of Holy Week. It is supposed to represent the mother of the Lord in pain and sorrow and is used on Good Friday at the fourth Station of the Cross. Some moradas also feature statues of Saint John or Maria Magdalena. On both sides of the alter are placed wooden candleholders. In the background different paintings of the Passion are visible. The colors for the paintings are produced naturally from the juices of plants and trees. Rarely will one find pictures of the fourteen stations in the morada, but instead small crosses hang from the walls, each representing one station.

A door leads into a second room with poor lighting. The furnishings consist of a tiled stove, a table and a few benches and are used as conference room, dining room, and resting place. That is all. Quite often one can see in front of the morada a dozen heavy, crudely hand-made crosses of different sizes. The number of crosses varies depending on the number of members of each morada. The crosses are twelve feet long and the cross beam is five feet wide. Such a cross is very heavy and needs a strong man to drag it along.

There are differences in architectural styles of moradas depending on their locations. Some moradas are attached to the Catholic Church, as is the case in Las Trampas, one of the Peñasco missions. The altar's age in Las Trampas is estimated to be three hundred years. The exact date of the construction of the church is unavailable as no records survived. Documents considered significant to the construction of the church were scrutinized and turned out to be irrelevant. Popular belief has it that the first settlers consisted of twelve families who constructed the church. Its adobe walls are four feet thick and the walls are more than twenty feet high. The church is 120 feet long and 30 feet wide. The beams of the flat roof are massive and rest on hand carved corbels which are safely embedded into the adobe walls. The entire floor is made of massive old wood and is designed to look like graves. In the steer of the church are two altars decorated with scenes from the bible. The sanctuary consists of two separated parts—for one, a barandal or communion bench. Three steps up is the actual sanctuary where the main altar is located. The altar is as old as the church itself and made entirely of raw wood.

On each side of the altar is a nook and behind the altar a wall rises to the beams covered with paintings of old saints. The paintings are artistic expressions of the original residents of Las Trampas. The colors of the paintings are still fresh. In the wooden tabernacle of the altar, an old two-part monstrance is preserved. When screwed together, it measures two feet high. The monstrance is likely from Spain. There is also an old goblet in the tabernacle. The current priest found this dusty goblet, restored it according to the rules of the church, and now uses it in celebrations. It is said that the goblet was cast in town, but that is difficult to verify.

Covering on the side of the altar is an old wooden board, which unfortunately has been painted over and thus the inscriptions are nearly illegible. Some of the words indicate that the altar was exceptional despite the crude wood work. Two old whimsical wooden statutes covered with calico and laces are found on the other side of the altar. They are the statues of the Virgin Mary and Saint John. For years the church at Las Trampas was heavily visited in los rincones [parish, district], only second to the one in the Indian village of Picuris. Still today during times of great summer droughts, it is tradition among Spanish Americans to take the statues and carry them in processions across the fields asking God's blessing for a good harvest.

No stranger is allowed to enter the church because of its old and precious antiquities, unless given permission. In that case two Penitentes have to accompany the visitor. Fifteen years ago a hand-made old confession bench, perhaps the only one of its kind in New Mexico, disappeared. Still today, the church owns a hand-carved pulpit carried by a single spiral column. The priest generally gives his sermon from the altar, but once a year, on the day of the Corpus Christi procession in Las Trampas, he steps up to the pulpit with the help of a ladder provided for this event.

The strangest place in the church is the baptismal chapel, which Penitentes use often during lent. As soon as the visitor enters the church, his sight falls on the wall just below the old organ choir which incidentally has to be accessed with a ladder. The wall is decorated with carvings and paintings representing Native American symbols and their interpretation is a study in and of itself. On the right-hand side is a strange old hand-carved door hanging on wooden hinges. Once inside, there is the baptismal basin built from massive stone. The surface is covered with copper inlay. There is also a deathbed (which reminds this writer of his first funeral in the Indian pueblo of Picuris in 1920).

During that Indian funeral, the priest awaited the body in front of the church. But how surprised was he, once the procession came closer, to see that the body was wrapped in Indian blankets and carried by four Indians on an old ladder. The body was so tightly wrapped and tied with thin ropes that the form of the body was easily recognizable. The body was turned over to the priest, carried into the church, and then placed on a specially prepared table. After the mass, the priest accompanied the body to its final resting place. There, he expected to see a casket waiting, but to his disappointment, there was none. When he glanced down into the grave, he noticed at one end a small excavation in form of a human head and understood the situation: the body was buried in its present form and gave the appearance of a living person being buried.

Later, upon return to the sacristy, the priest called for the sacristan and the Governor of the Pueblo to take them to task about the funeral procedure and subsequently to prohibit this kind of burial. The priest was told that this was the traditional way of burial and could not be changed. Today it is no longer applied and instead a casket is used.

Something particularly remarkable is the death cart which Penitentes use in the procession during lent. The death cart is old, crudely built and very low riding. Between the two heavy wheels is a small raised seat on which a skeleton is positioned. The carved wooden face of the figure is long and narrow, white as a wall, and with the teeth implanted, to look like a real skull. The rest of the body of this sitting and grinning figure is covered with an old black cloth, only to allow a peek at the bony skeleton feet. In the left skeleton hand, the figure is holding a bow, and in its right one an arrow ready to shoot. The cart has a shaft placed in the center with which it can be pulled. This all represents a primitive presentation of death and teaches the danger of unexpected death.

[Küppers, obviously absent-minded, returns here to his description of the Las Trampas church.] In a corner of this room, a few chains and things like matracas [wooden rattles] are laying around, which are used during the Tenebrae [last three eves of Holy Week]. It has been rumored that the walls of the room are splattered with human blood at the end of Lent. That might have been true in the past, but is no longer the case today. There is also a big triangle candleholder which holds six candles on each side and one at the tip. This room is a good example of past ceremonies of the Penitentes.

The church of Las Trampas is surrounded by a cemetery which is still in use today. In the past, however, influential Mexicans and Spanish Americans were buried inside the church and, according to elders in the village, had to pay dearly for such a privilege. One of the graves at the foot of the altar contains the remains of a priest. Legend among the villagers has it that Las Trampas was for years the parish seat, but this is doubtful, as Picuris is the parish residence since 1640. The individual graves inside the church are easily recognizable by the massive wooden floor panels which separate each grave.

The church of Las Trampas had two bells, both cast in town. Two to three hundred years ago in New Mexico, the villagers themselves made bells. To buy bells in Mexico City and transport them to New Mexico was almost impossible. Self-help is the best help, and thus, a so-called horno or oven was built from adobe in form of the desired shape of the bell. This horno had two walls and between the walls the liquid metal was poured. Next to the oven a copper kettle was placed to receive the hard metal. It was an honor for the Spanish women to throw their gold and silver jewelry and ornaments into the kettle. Then the kettle was closed airtight, and only a pipe led from the kettle to the oven. A steady hot fire was maintained around the kettle, and as soon as the metal began to melt, it ran into the cast of the bell in the horno.

There it remained for a day and then, as part of a big celebration, the horno was broken up and the finish bell was heaved into the bell tower. The ringing then was produced by means of a stone. It is such a pity that so many of the oldest churches and chapels sold these bells to curio merchants. Of the two bells that rang in Las Trampas, only one is left today; the other one was stolen in 1921, broken up in pieces, and offered for sale in Denver, Colorado. Unfortunately, the metal pieces did not contain the expected amount of gold and silver, and therefore returned to the sender. That is how the thief was discovered. The bell that remains is valuable and contains much gold, silver, and copper as the jewelry of the Spanish doñas was melted into the bell.

The morada is attached to the right of the church and in front of it a few crosses are placed on the ground. The interior of the morada does not distinguish itself from any other morada: a room with an altar, and another room for gatherings of private matters. In the parish of Peñasco the Corpus Christi procession is traditionally conducted three times: on Corpus Christ Sunday in Peñasco, on the second Sunday in Las Trampas, and on the third Sunday in Embudo. In Las Trampas, four altars are erected in the church yard. Four posts are hammered into the ground for each altar, and this square is covered with beautiful Mexican blankets. Inside the square a table is set up, which serves as the altar. Flowers if available, otherwise branches of cedar and fir, titivate the altar. The path of the procession is also lined with fir branches.

The priest conducts the High Mass and the church is overflowing with people, many of whom have traveled from nearby missions to attend the celebrations. A small portable harmonium provides the church music which is needed at every altar for the blessing. High Mass then is followed by the sermon which is delivered from the old pulpit. Thereafter the procession begins. The most sacred Host is held in the old voluminous monstrance. A Penitente leads the procession carrying the heavy cross and is followed by the Penitentes' banner and all the members of the brotherhood who continuously sing Penitentes hymns during the walk. The situation has an amiable feel of the medieval ages. Behind the Penitentes then, follow in long lines the remaining people, a few children in white dresses, and the priest with the Patron Saint sheltered under a canopy of white linen. Behind the priest trail the sexton and server—also a Penitente—carrying an old censer. Everything is rather primitive except the good people's belief, which is very much alive.

It is a condicio qua non [duty] for every Penitente to observe lent. He, who cannot commit to it, can no longer be a Penitente. He is ipso facto [matter of fact] suspended, and can only be reinstated after he has fulfilled his obligations. New members, too, have to be registered with the priest, and only he decides ultimately on their admission. Every Easter Monday is a Penitentes mass in the church or chapel that is home to the Hermano major. All members of the morada are expected to attend and the priest gives an overview of the past year's activities. Praise and censure where appropriate, are given to each morada. After mass, the Penitentes will proceed to their morada, and if private matters need to be discussed, this is the time to do so. After business matters are concluded, a communal lunch is served during which nobody speaks other than a Penitente, generally the resador [in charge of hymns and prayer] who reads from a religious book until lunch is over. The priest then says his good-byes and at dawn he accepts the Penitentes' main banner for safe keeping in the church.

It is incorrect to think that all moradas are alike. There are three categories to consider. The first category of moradas does not allow any penitence or exercises, not even carrying of the cross. Members of those moradas limit themselves to service in the church and prayer alone. That is the case with the two moradas in Embudo. When at the beginning of lent elections for a new Hermano Major occur, the list of candidates is presented for approval to the priest. The priest, then, will announce the program for lent, and each morada can schedule its own programs around it to avoid conflicts. All members have to attend services as well as the services of the Penitentes. This category of moradas, obviously, is easily acceptable to the church, even recommended as a kind of male congregation. Members of these moradas are of great help to the church, particularly during lent.

The second category of moradas are those that still pursue penances in secrecy. Mild flagellations are tolerated such as cross carrying after dark or in a non-public place during daytime. Never are fanatic flagellations allowed, not even in secrecy. Usually on Friday afternoons during lent, when the priest is unable to be present, in some instances the Stations of the Cross are done under the open sky, even with a very heavy cross ahead of the procession; but no flagellations occur. This second category is not prohibited by the church ["but tolerated" is crossed out in manuscript].

The third category of moradas is one whose members only minimally dressed, participate in public flagellations and public cross carrying. These situations are offensive and those who provoke them cannot be receiving the Holy Sacraments of the Church. Usually, observers of those exercises blame the Church and wonder how can the Catholic Church tolerate such behavior? The church does not condone these exercises and never has. To the contrary, it renounces this unworthy behavior very strongly. The number of such moradas [belonging to this 3rd category] is on the decline and will soon be a memory. Church authorities and the priests have always opposed these flagellations. They fight this conduct currently, have in the past, and will do so in the future.

The first two categories of moradas are well organized, though the first one is in better order than the second. Nobody will be admitted whose lifestyle is in doubt. Reciprocal protection and care of families, upstanding morality and obedience toward the Church are of utmost importance to each member. In the opinion of this writer, members of those moradas are of great benefit to the Church. They often represent a stronghold against the creeping influence of Protestantism among Spanish Americans, particularly against Protestant schools and Protestant education. Many villages have resisted the propaganda of Protestant teachers and pastors, because the brotherhoods were well organized. Ever since the propaganda of Protestantism is at work, living conditions among the Spanish population have deteriorated rather than improved.

Rules and Admissions Regulations into the Morada

No unity among the Penitentes at large in New Mexico exits. This is a pity as in its unity lays the preservation of the Penitentes. Were the Penitentes united under one umbrella organization, they would represent, if schooled properly in the spirit of the church, a powerful entity in clerical life. As for right now, it depends on the priest to educate each morada in the clerical views. This writer may be optimistic but his own experience confirms this view. Leadership has to exist in every organization as well as obedience among its members. Once that is achieved, the foundation of the organization is secured. This is also true for the Penitentes.

Who is better suited to provide leadership in a brotherhood than the Catholic priest? Without his leadership, brotherhoods inevitably move slowly toward their demise. Penitentes understood this clearly in the last few years and acted accordingly. If the group wants to be accepted as a clerical organization then the priest is the leader of the Penitentes in his parish. The priest has charge of the morada and can enter it at anytime. It is the priest who decides membership in and dismissal from the morada. The priest can decide over all questions in his parish and this makes a continuous clerical organization possible. The leading Penitentes are aware of this and therefore moradas seek more and more of his advice and help.

A good example is the well organized morada in Taos, famous for its art colony. Taos is the center not only of all moradas in Taos County but also for most of the moradas in the north and in the south. To the north, there are brotherhoods in the parish of Costilla and in the south those of Peñasco. The center or *el centro* has authority over all moradas that subordinate themselves to it. The election of its leaders is conducted every year on 15 August. Each morada sends representatives with voting rights. Obedience and subservience of the members to their leaders in all administrative aspects are the primary conditions. The administrative leader of the center is the Hermano Major del Centro who has nearly omnipotent power with respect to his members. He is assisted by three conciliarios or councilors among whom the conciliario general is most influential. The three conciliarios, in turn, are aided by three aconsejeros or advisers who, too, have to be consulted in important decisions. These seven men hold in their hands the well-being of all moradas belonging to the center. Their decisions are final and have to be accepted by each member, if he doesn't want to lose membership in his morada. The secretario del centro who keeps minutes of all gatherings and decisions made and who administers the center's correspondence, has no vote. The same is true for the tesorero who is responsible for monetary matters. Every member of each subordinate morada contributes a small amount of money each year to maintain the brotherhood. The leaders of the center are required to visit and inspect each morada once a year. If irregularities occur that cannot be resolved within the morada itself, the center's decision is final. The visit usually happens during lent and is called mission. Generally the priest is asked to celebrate mass which has to be attended by all members. Difficulties and approbations of decisions are brought to the attention of the priest after mass.

The organizational structure of a morada is simple. At the top is the Hermano Major who is entrusted with the overall leadership of the morada. With a conciliario and an aconsejero at his side, he is responsible for each individual member. Everything that is of interest to the Morada or pertains to its individual members is of their concern. In earlier times, the Hermano Major appointed a co-adjutor who was responsible for the crosses and disciplinas [instructions]; the adjutor or helper also had to keep the morada in good condition, and if work on the morada was necessary, he made sure that each member was assigned his share of work.

[Peter Küppers inserted here a glossary of morada terms:]

Celador or zealot [actually monitor]. It is the monitor's duty to watch members' moral standings and should one fail in his personal life, to bring him before the Hermano Major. It is also his responsibility to recruit new members.

Secretario or clerk. He is in charge of the rules and regulations of the brotherhood and maintains the fiscal books. He also keeps proper minutes of everything that is said or done in gatherings.

Tesorero or treasurer—monetary affairs

Enfermero or nurse—if a Penitente falls ill, it is the nurse's duty to inform members, and to decide if the sick member is in need of help. He will arrange for night watch should it become necessary.

Maestro de Novicios or Master of Novices. His position is the second most important one after the Hermano Major's. It is the Maestro's task to instruct those who intend to enter the Morada permanently. Attitudes of those newly chosen depend to a great extent on the Maestro, who is usually one of the older and wiser Penitentes. Because novitiate lasts at least one year, the Maestro's task is the most difficult one.

Coadjutor or Segundo Hermano Major is the person who assists the Hermano Major and fills in during his absence. He has the same responsibilities as his superior.

Mandatario or Commander. It is this person's duty to inform Penitentes of ordinary and extraordinary meetings in the morada. If a call for action is necessary, the Mandatario will notify the Penitentes. He is the page of the Penitentes.

Resador: In charge of hymns of praise as well the prayer.

Pitero: He plays the flute during private and public events. A pito is a flute and is used generally during Penitentes' processions. However, not all moradas still use the pito as it attracts, with its shrill, atonal, and piercing sound, too much the attention of the public. Because of its unique sound, one knows immediately where the Penitentes are and the result is that many curiosity seekers assemble. That is why many moradas discontinued the position of the pitero, and those who still retain this position make seldom use of it.

Hermano de la Caridad: Brother of Love, or even better, charity. In the past this brother was also called Sangrador [blood letter] or Pricker [someone who 'pierces or pricks] and could be found in old tales about the hermandad. Today the name Sangrador is no longer in use and replaced with the nicer sounding name Hermano de la Caridad, Brother of Charity. His duty is to place the seal or Sello of brotherhood on the newly admitted brothers. After the Third Order of St. Francis was dissolved, the seal was introduced by unscrupulous politicians who took over the leaderless brotherhoods. It is difficult to change that situation. Much has been written about the seal—mostly in exaggeration. The truth is that the Hermano de la Caridad takes the so-called pedernal—a short pointed stone like an arrowhead produced from a special kind of stone [likely flint]—and hands it to the new Penitentes as the seal of the order.

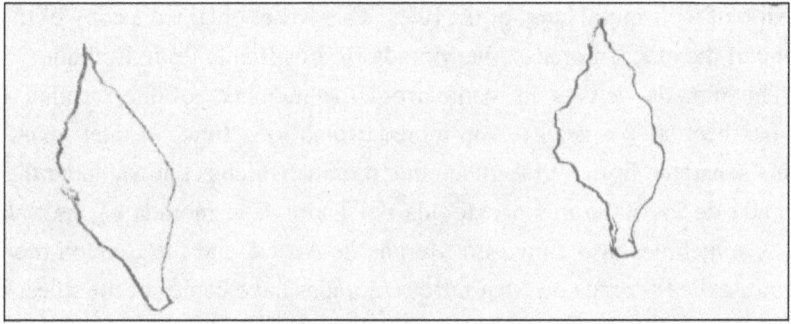

Father Peter Küppers's original sketch of a *Pedernal*—an arrowhead shaped stone—possibly given to new Penitentes. Reproduced from Küppers's notes.

With the seal, three parallel running cuts, one to two inches long, are incised above the loin into the flesh on both sides of the body. Often two [actually three—based on Küppers's own drawings] perpendicular running cuts had been added. The cuts which are cleaned immediately afterwards, are not very deep and almost painless. The cuts are often so superficial that not even blood is running. The cuts are done in the manner below.

Father Peter Küppers's original sketch of three horizontal and three vertical cuts possibly incised into the flesh of a Penitente as a symbol of membership. Reproduced from Küppers's notes.

It is not true that the cuts have to be exposed during all of lent. The ritual was performed only once and not, as is so often reported, during every lent. In the past, when a Penitente requested access to an unknown morada, he had to show his sello. If he did not have one, he was not admitted.

The rules of the Confraternidad de Nuestro Padre Jesus date back to 27 October 1856. The Archbishop of Santa Fe at the time, Juan B. Lamy, drew them up in Santa Fe and imposed them on the Penitentes. The Church only acknowledges those moradas that accept the rules and obeyed them. The authentic document can no longer to be found, not even in the archives of the Archdiocese in Santa Fe. Every morada received the rules or made a copy of them. Still today, most moradas are in possession of their initial copy of the rules. This writer obtained a copy of the rules from one of the oldest moradas, the Morada De Los Rendones in Embudo.

The morada derives its name from the members of the Rendon family which has been at the head of the morada for a long time. In later years many members separated from it to form another morada which is known under the name La Morada de los Salazares or Morada del Padre. The morada of the Salazares family is sometimes also called La Morada de Arriba, and the Rendon morada is sometimes called Morada de Abajo. Both moradas have copies of the rules. Today, the Morada de Los Salazares has more members than the Morada de Abajo, 33 and 16 respectively. The copy of the rules, which this writer has in front of him, was produced on 25 March 1859.

Here are the rules of the brotherhoods of the Penitentes who run under the name F.P.D.N.P.J.N.[1]

> Pious Confraternity of Our Father Jesus, The Nazarene
> To the greater Honor and Glory of God
>
> Rules that have to be observed by the Brothers of the Catholic Fraternity of Penance
>
> Rule No. 1
> Nobody can be received into this Brotherhood who does not profess the Catholic, Apostolic Roman Religion.
>
> Rule No. 2
> Anyone who wishes to join this Brotherhood will have to present his petition

to the Hermano Major who after examining the petition will rule upon the acceptance of the Candidate or not. If affirmative, he will name two brothers, in whom he has all confidence to get information of the moral conduct of the applicant. If nothing infamous results against the postulant he can be admitted and taken over by the master of novices, who during the years has to study him attentively and conscientiously and who has to watch over his inclinations. In case he discovers grave faults who [sic] prove to be incorrigible he has to reveal these to the Hermano Major, to the Celadores and the other officials of the Brotherhood, so that they themselves may observe the conduct of the novice. When sure that this is in conformity with the statements of the Master of novices, he will not be permitted to form a part of the Brotherhood.

Rule No. 3
All the brothers will keep the secret concerning business affairs discussed in the meetings. The Hermano Major is obliged to notify the Parish Priest so that he may assist and preside at all the meetings, if he wishes to do so. If one of the brothers would break the secret, he will be severely corrected according to the disposition of the Hermano Major and the Celadores and if falling back into the same fault will be expelled from the Brotherhood.

Rule No. 4
As it is required that every member of the Brotherhood be morally good and virtuous to incite by his good example others to virtue it is prescribed and ordered that when a brother gives scandal against the sixth, seventh and second law of God (which is blasphemy), he will be severely punished by the Hermano Major and the Celadores for the first offense and when repeated shall be expelled from the Brotherhood.

Rule No. 5
All the brothers who took part as members of the Brotherhood and who were not for any other offense excluded from the Brotherhood and who have not committed any other offense against any other of the preceeding [sic] rules can, if they wish to, return to be a member again of the Brotherhood.

Rule No. 6
If anyone ever expelled makes a claim to be admitted again, he will be

recived [sic] after a prudent investigation that has proven that he has mended his ways, but if he reliquishes [sic] again he will be forever expelled from the Confraternity

Rule No. 7
The Hermano Major, the Celadores and the Helpers in every question arising among the brothers are authorized to keep order and see that all obligations are complied with. The first Helper in all questions and matters [shall] be the one to pronounce sentence and that he will inform the Parish Priest by means of a cicise [concise], clear and true statement of what has taken place exposing circumstances and derelicts.

Rule No. 8
Every one who belongs to the Brotherhood must receive the Sacraments of Penance and the Holy Eucharist especially during Lent and if someone does not comply he will be forever expelled without being admitted again in the future.

Rule No. 9
All and every one of the members of the Brotherhood must obey and respect the legitimate and Supreme Pastor of this Territory, His Excellency the Most Rev. Catolic [sic] Bishop Juan Lamy and His Successors in everything they find good to command. The same obedience must be rendered to the Parish Priest or to any other of the Diocese appointed by the Bishop without complaint and murmur. After disobeying the second time, the member must be expelled from the Brotherhood as unworthy of a Catholic congregation, whose fundamental bais [bias] are obedience and Charity.

Rule No. 10
Concerning the preceeding rule obedience and respect to the Parish Priest is required. However he being responsible directly to the Prelate everything that might happen in the Brotherhood like abuses by some members, the Hermano Major has the obligacion [sic] to deliver a list of all persons belonging to the Brotherhood to the Priest so that he can answer any time to everything that might be said by people of bad will against the good name of the Brotherhood.

Rule No. 11

Every Hermano Major must have a copy of the original of these rules signed by the Parish Priest without permitting however that more copies than necessary are made to avoid a change of the rules or adulteration of the original unintentionally by through fault of the writers. Each copy must be written the same and signed by the Parish Priest.

Rule No. 12 and last

All those rules must be manifested to all members so that they know them. In order not to become forgotten, should be read from time to time. Nobody is allowed to interprete [sic] the rules his own way but must be taken verbally. In case of doubt recourse must be made to the Parish Priest and he in turn with the Prelate. The same must be done if something has to be added or left out according to circumstances.

According to the rules, the Bishop's admonition is followed in the words of St. Tomas: "Dadme un Superior que a la sanctidadreune la virtud de la prudencia y una comunidad estara bien arreglada." ("Give me a superior who combines the virtue of wisdom with Holiness, and a community will remain in good order"). It is clear from the Spanish copy, that the first man to copy out the rules, a certain Jose E. Ortiz, made many mistakes. Archbishop Lamy not only understood, but wrote and spoke Spanish fluently just like his French native language.

It is the task of the Maestro de Novicios to familiarize the new Penitentes with the rules so to introduce them to the importance of the Morada.

Ceremony of Acceptance. After the necessary instruction and the final exam, acceptance into the morada is imminent. All members gather in the morada, only the hopeful future members or aspirants are waiting outside. Every novice, one after another, has to go through the same ceremony, the Afuera [coming out]:

> Now the Hermano de la Caridad rises and steps with the new brother into the second room to give him the seal of the brotherhood. In the past, this may have been a harsh ordeal, but nowadays it does not amount to much. Some moradas no longer use the seal. As mentioned earlier in this chapter, the procedure is done with a sharp stone, the pedernal. The Hermano de la Caridad takes the stone and cuts into the exposed part of the novice's body: three short lines and often two additional perpendicular lines are cut into both

sides of the loin. If any blood appears at all, it is immediately cleaned out, but usually it is only a ceremony reminding of past traditions. This ceremony now behind him, the former novice is now a full Penitente.

***

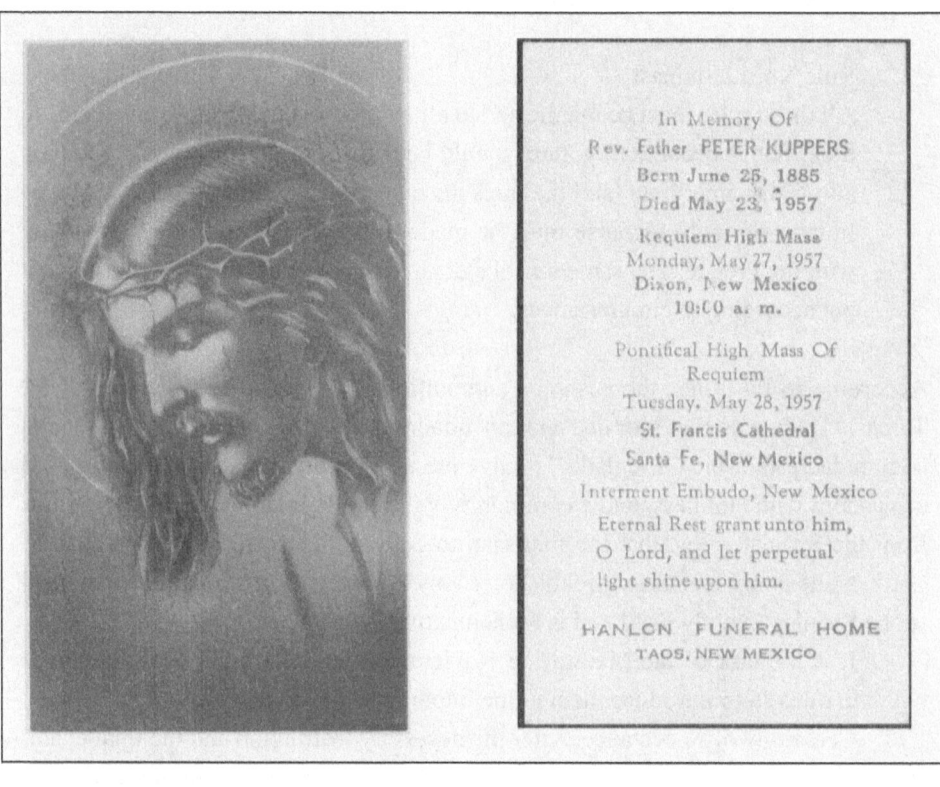

Father Küppers's Memorial Card. He died on 23 May 1957. Courtesy the Author.

Appendix

[Article reproduced here with permission of the publishers appeared in *Seeds of Struggle, Harvest of Faith: The Papers of the Archdiocese of Santa Fe Catholic Cuarto Centennial Conference on the History of the Catholic Church in New Mexico* (Albuquerque: LPD Press, 1998), pp. 291-310]

The Priest who made Schools Bloom in the Desert: Peter Küppers, 1911–1957

On 10 March 1949 the *Santa Fe New Mexican*'s front-page headline read: "Suit Demands Removal of Nuns From Public School Positions." Many New Mexicans still remember the so-called "Dixon Case,"[1] wherein a group of citizens sought to ban all Catholic nuns and priests, who had taught Catholic doctrine in New Mexico from teaching in the public schools. The controversy, in local and national news until the final ruling by the New Mexico Supreme Court of 1951, signaled a new era of separation between New Mexico's religious and public education. Archbishop Edwin V. Byrne (1943–1963) withdrew the religious teachers. Otherwise, the Dixon case would have had, as historian Ferenc Szasz has noted, "the potential to become a national Supreme Court pathbreaker."[2]

Few, however, have ever heard of Peter Küppers, resident of Dixon and parish priest of Peñasco-Dixon in Northern New Mexico from 1921 to 1934. At the time of the lawsuit he had already retired and was living on his fruit farm "Obscurana." During his tenure in the Peñasco-Dixon parish, he actually initiated the climactic controversy by building the first Catholic school and continued to play a part in the issue until 1951. Highly regarded among poor as well as politically influential Hispanics, and friend to many well-known Anglos of the time, this obscure immigrant from Germany wielded momentous influence over not only the educational and spiritual well-being of New Mexicans but on their political and social lives as well. He carried so much influence in Northern New Mexico that a differently minded fellow priest in the early 1930s called him the "Clerical Huey Long" and "Czar of Dixon."³ In 1947, a reader responding to the *Time* article on the Dixon controversy, "Compromise in Santa Fe," still identified Küppers as one "who once ruled Dixon like a dictator and is still able to wield great political power behind the scenes."⁴

Küppers's significant political and social authority was fueled by his passion for the Hispanic people of Northern New Mexico and by his decidedly Catholic understanding of education. The young priest's grasp of the importance of the Church's role in education ran contrary to the opinions of many Anglo-Americans at the time. Poverty in New Mexico resulted from the fact, so their argument ran, that the Catholic Church kept the Spanish-speaking population ignorant "of reading, arithmetic, and other social and economic skills necessary for survival in the Anglo-American world."⁵ In letters, essays, and in his memoirs Küppers reiterated his convictions on Church-sponsored education. In an undated, unpublished paper "Religious Situation in New Mexico," Küppers explained, for instance, that assimilation to the Anglo-American culture required faith in the high ideals of Catholicism: "Give [the Spanish American] ... a good religious training and he will surpass all expectation in [Anglo-American] progressivism."⁶ Considering that New Mexico's school system was still underdeveloped, Küppers may have grasped the situation like many other priests since Archbishop Lamy and tried to seize an opportunity to let the Catholic Church shape public schooling.⁷ Because he passionately believed that Hispanic children, particularly in rural districts, needed a good Catholic-public education, Küppers emphasized on numerous occasions that "the highest goal of my ecclesiastical work among Spanish American children, who are often simply called Mexican, [is] to give what all children needed most: a good education." ²

His uncompromising devotion also caused Peter Küppers to become a highly controversial figure within the Archdiocese. His methods for soliciting money and material for schools, recruiting teachers, and maintaining school buildings were often arguable, and reprimands from the Archdiocese in Santa Fe ranged from friendly criticism to outright chastisement. It depended who was in power. Archbishop Jean Baptiste Pitaval (1909–1918) had a somewhat tense relationship with Küppers, while Archbishop Albert Thomas Daeger (1919–1932), a man Küppers called " New Mexico's greatest and most humble archbishop," offered merely friendly, fatherly criticism. Daeger's successor, Rudolph Aloysius Gerken (1933–1943), kept Küppers's practices under close scrutiny. An increasing conflict between those two, combined with accusations of embezzlement and immorality against Küppers, led ultimately to Küppers's removal from his position as parish priest in Peñasco in December 1934. This chapter in the German priest's life may never be adequately resolved but remain instead a myth of part gossip and part truth. And even an attempt to solve some of the controversy surrounding Küppers would go beyond the scope of this paper. Nevertheless, it should not detract from his service to the people in New Mexico.

Therefore, this paper will be limited to a brief sketch of his life to give sufficient background to tackle his significant influence on Hispanics' education and spiritual life in Northern New Mexico. Primary sources for this paper come from the Historic-Artistic Patrimony and Archives of the Archdiocese of Santa Fe. There I found a draft of a typed autobiography, personal papers, parish files and a few personnel files. The New Mexico Archives and Record Center and the Museum of New Mexico also provided information about Küppers. In addition, I undertook several very rewarding field trips in San Miguel County and in the Peñasco-Dixon area where I gathered some oral history. I also located relatives of Küppers in Santa Clara, California, and in his birthplace in Germany.

Peter Küppers was born on 25 June 1885 in Kückhoven, Germany, the eldest of 14 children. His father was overly strict and his mother died when he was in his early teens. He did not get along with his father's second wife, and soon left home for good. His autobiography indicates that his career choices were carpentry, his father's business, or the priesthood. Apparently, Küppers chose the latter, and went to a seminary in Switzerland. The craftsmanship he picked up in his father's shop, though, would come in handy once he settled in New Mexico. In 1911, the year he was ordained in the Cathedral of Cologne, Archbishop Pitaval visited Europe and recruited Peter Küppers and several other graduates from the Swiss seminary.[9]

Küppers arrived in the United States in early 1912, and was "pretty furious that nobody in the United States spoke or understood German."[10] After a brief vacation in Pennsylvania, he undertook the long trip to New Mexico. Nothing in his memoirs or personal letters indicates that he was prepared for this country in any way. In his memoirs he recalls that "it was difficult to get used to the thought [of living in New Mexico], and the more I studied New Mexico's geography, the more subdued I became." Like most immigrants to New Mexico since the early 1840s, he was discouraged at first by the unfamiliar sight of adobe buildings and the poverty he encountered. He did not speak English or Spanish, nor was he familiar with New Mexican culture. Not surprisingly, comical situations arose, such as, when he held a sermon unwittingly in German for Spanish-speaking New Mexicans, or when he tried to communicate with prisoners at the penitentiary with little or no knowledge of English, or when he was tricked into eating his first bowl of chili.[11] His schooling in affluent Switzerland had not prepared him for the poverty and underdevelopment of New Mexico. What he brought with him, however, was a passion for people, a definite understanding of the value of education and distinct street smarts that would help him to succeed in his endeavors.

Once he arrived in Santa Fe, he adjusted quickly: "As Germans are used from childhood on to eat Sauerkraut and to follow it with a mug of beer or a glass of buttermilk, and as the Irish eat their potatoes unpeeled, and as the French have wine with their dumplings, I had to get acquainted with new habits."[12] In the relatively comfortable environment of Santa Fe, he began to learn the languages and customs of the land. His devotion for the Spanish American people was almost immediate and far more pronounced than that of other European newcomers. His first assignment as chaplain at the Guadelupe Church already demonstrates his activism and savvy in getting things done. When his parish priest was unfairly accused of pilfering the parish coffers, Küppers, with the help of some friends, managed to stall the proceedings, and to elect himself onto the church board, until he could present the accurate account books to the Archbishop.[13]

When funds were lacking to complete the Guadelupe rectory, a few friends explained to him how to make money in America. Through fund-raising efforts during the DeVargas procession and through theater performances, he collected $1000, enough to complete five rooms in the rectory and to install the first electric lighting in the church and rectory. By similar means he founded the Santa Fe chapter of the Knights of Columbus, furnished their home with former Palace Hotel furniture, and established a library for them.[14]

He became bolder on his first mission assignment. On 23 December 1913 Archbishop Pitaval appointed Küppers parish priest of Chaparito, an isolated community east of Las Vegas with fifteen missions spread across the vast plains of Eastern San Miguel County. The parish needed many improvements and he immediately began to fix buildings and build chapels in his missions. He worked hard to make the church in Chaparito more suitable, built chapels in La Garito and Sabinoso, and improved structures in Variadero and Los Torres. Küppers persuasively urged the local population to donate money and time to restore the 17th century chapel in St. Augustine. To improve the dismal education system, Küppers instructed his housekeeper to begin teaching school in Chaparito and Los Torres.

The dedicated housekeeper sold her house in Santa Fe to support maintenance of the missions, and also supplemented mission expenses with her state income as a schoolteacher.[15]

Education has always been a point of contention between Catholics and Protestants. Both churches viewed parochial schooling as the key to the future in New Mexico, which had, prior to the early 20th century, no school system to speak of. Each side began to set up parochial education programs; the Catholics worrying that public schools would be inevitably Protestant, and the Protestants fearing that the educational staff would be largely nuns and priests.[16]

Thus, it is not surprising that the presence of non-Catholic schools in Küppers's parish was a source of conflict for him, and his antagonism toward Protestant schools was already apparent in the 1910s in Chaparito. Although Protestant parochial schools provided their share of much-needed education, Küppers resented them as attempts to "wean" Catholic children and adults away from the faith.[17] So, like many of his contemporary Catholic priests, he tried to prevent Catholic children in his missions from attending the Protestant school in Trementina. With the help of influential politicians, he created new school districts and redrew the boundaries of established ones to put the Protestant school at a disadvantage. Once that was accomplished, he set out to improve education and find new and acceptable school buildings for his children.

With occasional help from villagers, he built a schoolhouse and converted the priest's residence into a sisters dormitory. On 15 November 1916 the new parochial school, which was to function as public school as well, was dedicated in Chaparito.[18] Now all he needed were sisters to teach. Archbishop Pitaval, though glad to see the Loretto Sisters come to Chaparito, cautioned Küppers "that it is very difficult, if not impossible, to get [sisters], for our poor missions."[19] Küppers's efforts to find sisters for Chaparito were indeed unsuccessful until he heard that sisters of a Spanish order were about evicted from Mexico and needed a new home. He saw his chance and accepted their offer to relocate without consulting with the Archdiocese in Santa Fe. Pitaval was irritated. The sisters did not speak a word of English, and Küppers's attempts to hide this small problem, only fueled Pitaval's anger. Furthermore, opposition began to form among the school board and locals. On 16 May 1917, less than six months later, Küppers wrote to Pitaval that "the parochial school at Chaparito was discontinued on account of the uncalled for, unfriendly attitude of Your Grace against my poor refugee sisters."[20]

That this "misunderstanding," as Küppers saw it, did not resulted in a serious reprimand, was due to Pitaval's general agreement with Küppers over the importance of Catholic schools. Pitaval strongly felt the need for Catholic schools; the lack of them was "the weak point in the Catholic fortress," as he pointed out in an address in 1909.[21] In Küppers's case, however, the archbishop had to consider the larger ramifications of New Mexico's official language of instruction, the laws for public schooling in general, and the image of the Catholic Church, which gave him little choice but to pressure Küppers to relieve the sisters.

Generally, the New Mexico statutes to secure public education had failed to make public education truly public and Küppers, in particular, was not really devoted to keeping public and parochial schools strictly separate.[22] Yet, at that time he blamed the sisters for the demise of the schools in Chaparito.[23] In his memoirs, some twenty-five years, later he apologized. Semi-ruefully, he admitted that perhaps he was most guilty because he wanted these non-English speaking sisters to teach public and parochial schools and, in turn, receive public funding.[24]

Prior to the departure of the sisters, Küppers convinced the state school board to set up an election for a bond to build a new public school building. A savvy lobbyist, he promoted the new school building during his Sunday services and tried to dissuade his enemies' argument that the capital outlay and interest for a new school bond would run extremely high. (Incidentally, he would reverse his position in Dixon some thirty years later, when the existence of his own school was at stake.[25]) He also attempted to persuade the sisters to vote should that be necessary for victory. The sisters, however, refused to vote feeling they needed special permission from their Provincial. In his disappointment and anger, Küppers himself forgot to vote and the bond for the school building failed.[26]

Küppers's tenure in Chaparito narrowly focused on Catholic education. Although Küppers knew that English was supposed to be the official language of instruction in public schools, he learned quickly that the law "was operating with marginal effectiveness over most of the territory."[27] He argued in his memoirs that the nuns were good teachers with sound methodology and the fact that they spoke little or no English was irrelevant; besides, this minor point could have been easily fixed with the School Board. He felt it was no different than the fact that "today teachers, and sisters included, don't speak Spanish but teach it in school."[28]

At Chaparito Küppers demonstrated his creative means to the perennial problem of funding Catholic schools and proved successful both in fundraising and politicking to improve schools and schooling.[29] His methods inevitably created tensions with his superiors. Pitaval reminded him more than once with "friendly advice" that he was "somewhat careless in business matters." Apparently Küppers did not heed the Archbishop's advice and Pitaval's letters became more stern: "[F]rom now on, you will do exactly what every other priest does, that is, settle all your accounts with the Chancery, as well as with the Ordinary, on or before the 1st of February of every year...."[30] In educational matters, too, Pitaval attempted to control Küppers's zealous activities: "Be it well understood, and I repeat it for the last time, that the work you intend to carry on, must be exclusively confined to your parish and missions.... In abiding by this understanding, and agreement, you will save your Archbishop, the pastor of Chaparito, and the sisters who came there upon your request, lots of trouble."[31]

Although Pitaval was concerned about some of the methods Küppers used, there is little indication of concern from Archbishop Daeger, who was appointed in 1919. A former parish mission priest in New Mexico himself, Daeger understood parish conditions and left local priests fairly free reign in handling their own affairs.[32] In addition, Küppers seems to have had a genuinely cordial relationship with his former fellow priest, now Archbishop, which benefited Küppers's almost fanatical quest to spread the Catholic faith, to provide education, and to minimize poverty among his parishioners.[33]

In 1921, against Küppers's wishes, Archbishop Daeger abruptly transferred his friend to the Peñasco mission—possibly because of an impending lawsuit over contested property between Küppers and locals. So, Küppers exchanged the wide-open rangelands of Eastern San Miguel County for the mountainous region of Taos and Rio Arriba Counties. There he continued his quest for better schools and education using methods similar to those he used in Chaparito. The school situation in the Peñasco parish was dismal when Küppers arrived. There was no school at all in Peñasco and only Presbyterian ones in Dixon and Chamisal. In 1922 he founded the first Catholic school in Dixon (which, along with the church he built in 1921, burnt down in 1928). He erected new school buildings, financed largely by himself and the Catholic Ladies of Columbus in Ohio.[34] In Peñasco, he opened a parochial and a public school with sisters in charge of both. In 1931, he opened a fully-accredited high school. While the county and state paid the sisters' salaries, the buildings and equipment belonged to the Archdiocese. State funds and donations from the East often paid for the maintenance of the schools. Daeger encouraged Küppers to make outside appeals for money and clothing, which the priest did with "tear-jerking form letters."[35] Soon, steady donations of money from the Catholic Ladies of Columbus became a reliable source of revenue. Since this northern New

Mexico area was a contested battlefield between Protestant, Catholic, and other faiths and since the Catholic Church feared the competition in education from the other denominations, Küppers's activities were condoned by his supervisors, and even encouraged.[36]

Within a short period of time in Peñasco, Küppers had built a political and social base among the local population and especially gained the support of the Penitentes, the Hispanic brotherhood of Northern New Mexico. The Penitentes have pledged themselves to Christian devotions without completely withdrawing from the daily world.[37] During Küppers's time in Peñasco, the Penitentes saw substantial changes. With the influx of many Anglo-Americans during the first decade of the 20th century, village life grew more heterogeneous. Outsiders intruded more and more often on Penitente rituals, seeing them as tourist attractions,[38] and the same rituals caused conflicts within the church hierarchy. Some of these customs persisted in New Mexico into the twentieth century, due in part to the extreme isolation of the people.[39] Küppers, like Archbishop Daeger, was familiar with and sympathetic toward the Penitentes, asking only that they conduct their exercises privately.[40] Daeger even requested that Küppers write a book on the Penitentes, and Küppers worked on a manuscript he had entitled "Mysteries of the Mountains." At some point he stated in a letter to Archbishop Gerken that the manuscript was ready and that he had plans to send it to the A. A. Knopf publishing house in New York.[41]

Küppers considered himself a confidant to the Penitentes who came to him for advice and counsel and whom he felt he could influence into following church rules. He said annual Masses and Funeral Masses for them "for nothing in some instances, for three dollars in others."[42] In turn, he was a staunch defender of their lifestyle. In fact, in his memoirs, he contended that the state of the Catholic faith in New Mexico would be better off if more Spanish Americans belonged to *moradas*.[43] They expressed their devotion to the Catholic faith, and their opposition to sending their children to Protestant schools.[44] He defended Penitentes against attacks from outsiders. When sensationalized publications appeared calling them fanatics or their ceremonies horrible, Küppers was quick to respond, defending them as law-abiding citizens, pious, well-meaning, and without any horrors in their ceremonies.[45] He described them as citizens of the United States who fought for their country in World War I, and as Spanish Americans who knew their Catholic religion. He also used his articles to plug the excellent schools in Northern New Mexico, and to attack Anglo-American deficiencies such as tenement housing in urban areas.[46]

Küppers remained loyal to the Penitentes throughout his life, even under

Archbishop Gerken, whose policy was more diplomatic and politically driven. When Küppers asked Gerken to endorse his forthcoming manuscript, the Archbishop replied that:

> "...since the book deals with the Penitentes of New Mexico, I will give you neither of the requested endorsements [Imprimatur or Nihil obstat], since, it might be detrimental. However, I will be glad to give my endorsement of the book, if the contents will not be objectionable to the Penitentes in general. Because, there are so many of these people in our Diocese, we will have to be very careful not to antagonize them unnecessarily."[47]

Küppers's successor in Peñasco apparently had his own misgivings about them saying that "the Penitentes are the greatest drawback to the spiritual uplift of the parish. [A]ll the preaching you do is in vain."[48]

Though the Penitentes represented a significant part of his power structure, Küppers never understood himself as taking a politically active role. In a letter to Governor Richard Dillon, responding to accusations that he had "mixed into politics," he wrote that a "Catholic priest should not mix into politics."[49] But contrary to his own perception, Küppers was highly political beyond the normal influence of a parish priest. In Chaparito he helped redraw school district boundaries. In Peñasco he asked for favors to place his parishioners in better paying state jobs, he tried to intervene on their behalf with judicial authorities, and he made his unsolicited opinions known to politicians on issues such as teachers' retirement funds and free textbooks.[50] His political influence was most pronounced on school issues. He tangled with the school board over parochial and state school issues, co-founded the Peñasco Independent School District, and became its first School Superintendent. This gave his adversaries excellent ammunition: "If a Priest is made Superintendent here and the schools remain independent of the County, the priest will be forced into politics at election times in order to oppose the candidates."[51]

Küppers's social position and political strength were secure among the Hispanic people in his parish, but his financial situation was not, despite donations and the State funds that Küppers controlled. On at least two occasions he requested the Archbishop's endorsement to divert public funds from the sisters' salaries directly to his schools. The Archbishop, though agreeing with the idea in principal, refused to endorse the proposal without the sisters' approval. Instead he counseled Küppers "to consider the trust, that is placed in you, as an official entitled to countersign checks, as most sacred, and that you pay the sisters according to their contract promptly, so that we will not bring any discredit upon the Church in our Diocese and state."[52] Ever since he accepted his first mission, Küppers controlled two nominally separate schools: a public school system and a parallel Catholic parochial system. For years the two systems overlapped in his parishes where funding was never enough for his ambitious school projects.[53] Under Daeger, Küppers fiscal matters were rarely scrutinized, but this changed when Daeger tragically fell to his death and Rudolph Gerken was appointed the new Archbishop of Santa Fe. While Küppers' behavior and methods always rose eyebrows in Santa Fe, it is not quite clear why the rift between him and Gerken was so immediate. Gerken's administration pursued "the American way" and kept much tighter control of his diocese than did his predecessors. He was also more forceful in his attempts to bring the Penitentes, one of Küppers's main support groups, in line with church doctrine.[54] Gerken questioned Küppers's practices at every turn and Küppers, who for decades had little outside supervision, took Gerken's concerns personally. That he may have entertained hopes of the Archdiocese himself could have put an additional strain on his relationship with Gerken.[55]

In any event, Küppers was not willing to accept Gerken's reign nor to follow his more decisive policy to separate church and state. Küppers refused to produce fiscal statements or legal documents on demand, and continued to amass debts to expand his programs at a time when the Depression kept monies tight in the church and communities. On numerous occasions, Gerken was forced to bail him out of his obligations.[56] Furthermore, Küppers stalled in visiting Gerken despite repeated requests from the Archbishop. His refusals to visit caused Gerken, in his letters, to put the phrase "when I see you next week" into quotation marks.[57] Küppers's unwillingness to see the Archbishop, combined with accusations by fellow priests that he was embezzling money for personal gain and that he was—as the Archbishop called it—"obligated to the two women" (his two long-time housekeepers) increasingly eroded his position within the clergy. In December 1934, Küppers was forced to resign from his post as parish priest and was prohibited from reading Mass.

Küppers withdrew from church life and settled down on his orchard "Obscurana" in Dixon. He continued to shape schools policy, as superintendent until January 1935, when he resigned for health reasons, and thereafter remained active in the schools as a private citizen.[58] He continued to write letters to political friends in Santa Fe on behalf of his former parishioners, to distribute clothing among the needy, and to help them fill out government forms. He also maintained contact with the Catholic Ladies of Columbus.[59] He improved his relationship with the Archbishop to the point that they exchanged cordial letters, written in German, and in early 1936 he was reinstated as priest of the newly created Dixon parish. Because he was still in ill health, he soon resigned this parish. Yet he remained active in the community and tended to his orchard. In 1957 he was taken to the hospital in Colorado Springs where he died on 23 March 1957, six years after the Dixon Case was decided and 35 years after he built his first school in Dixon.

What was Küppers's legacy? From a young inexperienced German priest, who learned the ropes in Santa Fe and Chaparito, he developed into an influential figure beyond the parishes of Peñasco and Dixon. As far as the records tell, he accepted the Northern New Mexican people wholeheartedly and without reservation and not as "an inferior breed of *pinto* sheep in the Lord's fold,"[60] the more common reaction Angelico Chavez ascribes to Northern European clergy. Early on Küppers promoted a policy of service, accommodation to cultural traditions, and social determination that put him ahead of many of his fellow priests.[61] He built and improved chapels, churches, and school buildings. At a time when there was little education, Catholic or otherwise, and the public school issue was still a gray area, Küppers took it upon himself to provide good education. When both Chaparito and Peñasco were still far removed from the politics of Santa Fe and Albuquerque, he created the political influence necessary for his projects to succeed. Ever in need of cash for his ambitious projects, Küppers occasionally mixed state funds, Catholic funds, private donations, and personal money, and not surprisingly called in political favors. In his zeal to succeed he created a few adversaries along the way among his own clergy and among Protestants, and probably he lost a few Hispanic friends as well.

In the 1930s, Küppers did not understand the changing sentiment that promoted further separation of church and state, and found it difficult to conform to rapidly changing policies in the Archdiocese. In this respect he resembles Padre Antonio Martinez, as one historian suggested, who "had been too long accustomed to be boss in his bailiwick, and had become too deeply enmeshed in his own casuistry to listen to the voice of reason."[62] Küppers himself felt he resembled Padre Martinez. In an unpublished essay he wrote about Martinez, conflict between priest and archbishop loom prominently and the priest's devotion to the local Hispanic community is conspicuous. Overall, Küppers saw Padre Martinez as a priest whose greatest talents went awry from the church, and, who should have received compassion rather than ostracism.[63]

In his eagerness to accomplish his visions, Küppers neglected to see that times had changed and public schools were understood to be no longer domain of a priest but of the public. The Dixon case symbolized New Mexico's "move away from a state where Roman Catholics dominated the religious and the political culture,"[64] when in 1951 the New Mexico Supreme Court upheld the ruling of the District Court and barred nuns, priests, and brothers from teaching in public schools of New Mexico. Although the Supreme Court did not disbar them as a class, Küppers finally had to acknowledge the change.

Notes

Preface

1. The spelling of this small hamlet is inconsistent and can be found in the historical literature as "Chaparito" and "Chaperito." I used "Chaparito" for the purpose of consistency.

My Educational Years

1. Die Echternacher Springprozession is a religious procession, which is performed each year on Tuesday after Pentecost weekend in Echternach, Luxembourg. Participants dance to polka melodies through the streets of the town to the grave of the Saint Willibrord in the Echternacher Basilika.
2. The "Convicte Salesianum" founded in 1907 as part of the University of Fribourg, housed theologians and future priests.
3. Exegesis (from the Greek εξηγεισθαι 'to lead out') involves an extensive and critical interpretation of a text such as the Old and New Testaments of the Bible, the Talmud, the Qur'an, etc.
4. Application of the general principles of rhetoric to public preaching.
5. Organization, founded in 1899, emphasized adult education with social-democratic values. The organization became outlawed in the Third Reich.
6. Adolf Braun, 1862–1929, active in the German labor movement and member of the Reichstag from 1920–1927. Carl Sonnenschein, 1876–1929, was active in the German labor and Socialist student movement in Germany. Dr. Nieder could not be identified.
7. Translation: "In memory of my beloved student Reverend Peter Küppers—Prof. Dr. Joseph Beck."

To New Mexico

1. John Baptist Pitaval, working in the Archdiocese of Santa Fe since 1902, was the archbishop from 1909–1918. He died in 1928.

Life in Santa Fe, New Mexico

1. During Küppers's times, chicory was commonly used in Germany in coffee substitutes.
2. Father Antoine "Antonio" Fourchegu was born in France in 1841 and arrived in the United States in 1867. He spent his entire clerical life in New Mexico having been ordained in 1868 by Archbishop Lamy. In 1911 he was appointed Monsignor by Pope Pius X at the request of Archbishop Pitaval. Monsignor Fourchegu died in Santa Fe in 1929 and is entombed under St. Francis Cathedral Basilica.
3. The linguistic equivalent to "This is all Greek to me" in German is "This is all Spanish to me" and frequently used by Küppers). This ethno-linguistic play on words is obviously missing the point in a Spanish-speaking place.
4. Eighty miles would be south of Albuquerque and north of Taos. Küppers is mistaken here. Perhaps it was a typographical error and he meant eighteen miles.

At the Cathedral

1. It seems that Küppers, in his convoluted German, indicated that the new presbytery had indoor plumbing.
2. This story is out of place. It is a story from the 1930s when Küppers was assigned to the Peñasco-Dixon parish. Küppers covers that period of his life in chapters 7-9.

To Chaparito

1. The sister may or may not have been the actual sacristan, but the 1917 Code of Canon Law allowed women to become sacristans.

2. The State Federation of Women's Clubs succeeded in providing women the right to school suffrage in 1910.

Soldiers of the Cross

1. New Mexico became part of Mexico in 1821 and its first governor was Francisco Xavier Chávez (1822–1823). Antonio de Narbona was succeeded by José Antonio Vizcarra (1825–1827).
2. A Vicar Forane, in general, did not have ordinary power to execute church laws.

The Penitentes of Today

1. Thank you to Josef Diaz, New Mexico History Museum, for his help in translating this letter into English.

Rules and Admissions Regulations into the Morada

1. Küppers lists the rules in Spanish and English; only the English version is displayed here. The rules appear to have been written down informally. His copy of the rules is based on Bishop Lamy's "Twelve Rules for the Brotherhood of Penance, October 27, 1856." A more formal and exact transcription of Archbishop Lamy's rules are reproduced in Marta Weigle, *Brothers of Light Brothers of Blood: The Penitentes of the Southwest* (Albuquerque: University of New Mexico Press, 1976), p. 201).

Peter Küppers, 1911–1957

1. The "Dixon case" was officially known as Zeller et al. v. Huff et al., No. 5332. *Report of Cases Determined in the Supreme Court and Court of Appeals of the State of New Mexico*, vol. 55 (St. Paul, MN: West Publishing Co., 1951), 501.
2. Ferenc M. Szasz, "The United States and New Mexico: A Twentieth Century Comparative Religious History," in Ferenc M. Szasz and Richard W. Etulain, eds., *Religion in Modern New Mexico* (Albuquerque: University of New Mexico Press, 1997), 187.
3. R.H. Lewis to Archbishop Gerken, 21 November 1934, PPF (hereafter PPF), Folder IV, Historic-Artistic Patrimony and Archives of the Archdiocese of Santa Fe, Santa Fe, NM (hereafter HAPA).
4. Arthur Montgomery to Editor of *Time*, 25 September 1947. Robert Jones Collection, Folder 3, "Dixon School Case, 1947–1950," State Record Center and Archives, Santa Fe, NM.
5. Randi Jones Walker, *Protestantism in the Sangre de Cristos, 1850–1920* (Albuquerque: University of New Mexico Press, 1991), 30.

6. Peter Küppers, "Religious Situation in New Mexico," Peter Küppers Collection (hereafter PKC), HAPA.
7. Susan M. Yohn, *Contest of Faiths: Missionary Women and Pluralism in the American Southwest* (Ithaca: NY: Cornell University Press, 1995), 77.
8. Peter Küppers, "Ein Deutscher Pfarrer in Neu Mexico" (A German Priest in New Mexico), Chapter "Nach Chaparito," 24. The typed manuscript is part of the PKC; it is a rough draft in German with many grammatical and syntactical errors.
9. Küppers was part of a trend of German secular clergy that began by 1880 to supplant the French clergy dominance in New Mexico. Nancy Nell Hanks, "Not of this Earth: An historical geography of French secular clergy in the Archdiocese of Santa Fe, 1850–1912" (Ph.D. diss., University of Oklahoma, 1993), 125.
10. "Deutscher Pfarrer," Chapter "Nach Neu Mexiko," 5-6.
11. "Deutscher Pfarrer," Chapter "Chapter 4," 1, 6, 7, 24.
12. "Deutscher Pfarrer," Chapter "Chapter 4," 1
13. "Deutscher Pfarrer," Chapter "Chapter 4," 17-21; newspaper clip, n.p., n.d., PKC.
14. Angelico Chavez, Index cards to Peter Kuppers's personnel file, HAPA; "Deutscher Pfarrer," Chapter "Chapter 4," 22-23.
15. In exchange, in his 1916 testament, Küppers deeded the proceeds of his life insurance policy ($3000) to his housekeeper.
16. Szasz, "Comparative Religious History," 185; Ferenc Morton Szasz, *The Protestant Clergy in the Great Plains and Mountain West, 1865–1915* (Albuquerque: University of New Mexico Press, 1988), 144.
17. Szasz, *Protestant Clergy*, 148-49.
18. Chavez, Index cards.
19. Pitaval to Küppers, 19 January 1915, PKC.
20. Deutscher Pfarrer," Chapter "Nach Chaparito," 41.
21. Jean Baptist Pitaval, quoted in Walker, *Protestantism*, 10.
22. Janice E. Schuetz, "A Rhetorical Approach to Protestant Evangelism in Twentieth-Century New Mexico," in Szasz and Etulain, eds., *Religion in Modern New Mexico*, 135.
23. "Statement concerning the state of affairs concerning the Sisters of Chaparito," 11 May 1918, PKC.
24. "Deutscher Pfarrer," Chapter "Nach Chaparito," 41.
25. Spanish circular, 24 August 1945, Robert Jones Collection, Folder 3, "Dixon School Case, 1947–1950."
26. "Deutscher Pfarrer," Chapter "Nach Chaparito," 37-8.
27. Szasz, *Protestant Clergy*, 148.
28. "Deutscher Pfarrer," Chapter "Nach Chaparito," 40; Chavez, Index cards.
29. Hanks, "Not of this Earth," 174.
30. Pitaval to Küppers, 16 December 1914, 21 March 1917, PKC.
31. Pitaval to Küppers, 10 November 1916, PKC.

32. Marta Weigle, *Brothers of Light, Brothers of Blood: The Penitentes of the Southwest* (Albuquerque: University of New Mexico Press, 1976), 102.
33. Marta Weigle, *Brothers of Light*, 101; Robert L. Wilken, *Anselm Weber, O.F.M.: Missionary to the Navahos, 1898–1921* (Milwaukee, WI: The Bruce Publishing Company, 1955), 147.
34. Küppers's $15,000 life insurance police covered some of the construction costs.
35. Albert T. Daeger, n.d., PPF 1934, Folder III; Chavez, Index cards.
36. Hanks, "Not of this Earth," 175-7.
37. Bill Tate, *the Penitentes of the Sangre de Cristos: An American Tragedy* (Truchas, NM: Tate Gallery, 1967), 10.
38. Weigle, *Brothers of Light*, xix, 96-97. For a recent interpretation of the Penitentes, see J. Manuel Espinosa, "The Origin of the Penitentes of New Mexico: Separating Fact from Fiction," *Catholic Historical Review* 79 (July 1993), 454-77.
39. Alice Corbin Henderson, *Brothers of Light: The Penitentes of the Southwest* (New York: Harcourt, Brace, and Company, 1937), 10. (New Edition. Santa Fe: Sunstone Press, 2013).
40. Weigle, *Brothers of Light*, 101.
41. Küppers to Gerken, 26 May 1934, PPF. Despite many references to the manuscript, the Peter Küppers Collection only contains fragments of a manuscript, and it appears the manuscript was never completed.
42. Lewis to Gerken, 20 March 1935, PPF.
43. Morada is the physical meeting place of the Penitentes or refers to the chapter as an organization of Brothers. See, Weigle, *Brothers of Light*, 239, ft. 17.
44. "Deutscher Pfarrer," "Soldiers of the Cross," 118.
45. Peter Küppers, Letter to the Editor, *St. Anthony Messenger*, 4 July 1938, in response to the publication by Phil Glanzer, *Religious Rites of Horror*.
46. Peter Küppers, "The Penitentes and *The Literary Digest*," *Southwestern Catholic,* 1921. Copy of the article in Dorothy Woodward Memorial Penitente Collection, Folder 110, New Mexico Records Center & Archives, Santa Fe, NM.
47. Gerken to Küppers, 31 May 1934, PPF 1934, III. Gerken commented about Alice Henderson's book *Brother of Light* that despite inaccuracies, "it is gratifying to see that the author endeavors to be fair to the Church and to the Penitentes. At any rate it could be much worse." Gerken to Küppers, 20 June 1938, PKC.
48. R. H. Lewis to Gerken, 20 March 1935, PPF 1935.
49. Küppers to Richard C. Dillon, 28 November 1928, PKC.
50. For example, Küppers to Miguel Otero, 17 June 1936, and Küppers to Epimenio Valdez, 20 February 1939; PKC.
51. Lewis to Gerken, 5 January 1934, PPF 1934, Folder IV.
52. Küppers to Gerken, 17 October 1934; Gerken to Küppers, 19 October 1934, PPF 1934, Folder V; Gerken to Küppers, 14 December 1934, PKC.

53. Ferenc M. Szasz, "Comparative Religious History," 186-7.
54. Weigle, *Brothers of Light*, 106.
55. Küppers to Joseph Beck (in German), 13 June 1936, PKC.
56. For instance, Küppers had owed over $5000 since 1932 to John P. Daleiden Company, Distributor of Religious Articles, Chicago, and Archbishop Gerken ended up paying the debt in 1935. Daleiden to Gerken, 25 April 1935, PPF 1935.
57. Gerken to Küppers, 3 January 1934, PKC.
58. Vertical File "Dixon Case," HAPA.
59. Form letter to the Catholic Ladies of Columbus (C.L.C.), 1 November 1948, PKC.
60. Angelico Chavez, *My Penitente Land: Reflections on Spanish New Mexico* (Albuquerque: University of New Mexico, 1974), 257. (New Edition. Santa Fe: Sunstone Press, 2012).
61. Carol Jensen, "Roman Catholicism in Modern New Mexico: A Commitment to Survive," in Szasz and Etulain, eds., *Religion in Modern New Mexico*, 3.
62. E. K. Francis, "Padre Martinez: A New Mexican Myth," *New Mexico Historical Review* 31 (October 1951): 281.
63. "Etwas über den berühmten Padre Antonio Jose Martinez," (Something about the famous Padre Antonio Jose Martinez), no date, PKC.
64. Schuetz, "Protestant Evangelism," 138.

www.ingramcontent.com/pod-product-compliance
Lightning Source LLC
Chambersburg PA
CBHW020052170426
43199CB00009B/260